THE POETICS OF GOLF

ANDY BRUMER

THE POETICS OF
GOLF

UNIVERSITY OF NEBRASKA PRESS • LINCOLN & LONDON

Acknowledgments for previously published
material appear on page 209, which constitutes
an extension of the copyright page.

Library of Congress Cataloging-in-Publication Data
Brumer, Andy.
The poetics of golf / Andy Brumer.
p. cm.
ISBN 978-0-8032-1365-4 (cloth : alk. paper)
ISBN 978-0-8032-7169-2 (paper : alk. paper)
1. Golf—Miscellanea. 2. Golfers. I. Title.
GV967.B875 2007
796.352—dc22
2007005771

Set in Minion by Kim Essman.

To the memory of my father

Contents

Preface

I've written poems and played golf for almost as long as I can remember and have enjoyed the ongoing struggle to master both activities. Through my practice I've discovered many similarities between poetry and golf, with the primary unifying principle being that they both pose "problems to be solved." Indeed, the solution to a specific swing problem that may have vexed me for some time often becomes clear to me in a dream, as if a great golf teacher were giving his or her lesson directly to me (in fact, they often do!). Likewise, images, ideas, or phrases for poems sometimes come to me in a dream all in a piece, and I wake up excited to write them down on a pad of paper next to my bed.

As a young man I wanted to become a great poet and a great golfer, though more than one sympathetic friend or family member pointed out to me the difficulty of making a living from either, let alone excelling in both! Therefore, although I've written and published poetry throughout my life, just as I've worked to improve my golf game from my days as a college player, I've also heeded reality's call by choosing to earn a living as a freelance arts and golf writer.

In a world of specialists, my work in multiple fields has raised eyebrows, and even I have felt confused at times as to where my true passion lies. A moment arrived when, rather than fight this division, I decided to integrate the two passions. As a wise friend of mine once said, "It's better to proceed through life via addition rather than subtraction." It is in this spirit that I began writing *The Poetics of Golf*.

This book does not argue that golf is literally poetry. Rather, it takes golf as its subject matter and a starting place for what aspire to be poetic essays, memoirs, journalism, short fiction, and other meditations on the game, the arts, and life.

For my title, I owe a nod of recognition to Aristotle's *Poetics* and to French writer and philosopher Gaston Bachelard's book *The Poetics of Space*. Aristotle's treatise explores how poetry's different genres imitate life, and it stands as a seminal work in the history of Western thought. *The Poetics of Space* discusses ordinary spaces, such as nests, corners, shells, drawers, and attics, with a marvelous intimacy and sensitivity to the way they reflect aspects of the human psyche and soul. Therefore, my book loosely uses the word *poetics* to signal a metaphoric and aesthetic investigation into the game of golf.

Many wonderful golfers, artists, and writers whom I've met along the way have joined me in these pages. Speaking for them, I'd like to invite you to journey with us now into golf's mysterious and inimitable poetry.

THE POETICS OF GOLF

1

Golf as Memoir

Taking It Back Inside

I waited until my mother had driven away. Then, after opening the front door, peeking down the road, and seeing her white Ford Falcon disappear, I lined up my eight-iron shot. Standing smack in the middle of the living room, with a plastic golf ball sitting on the carpet, I took dead aim through the small opening that skirted the chandelier and led through the back door to my target, a square of screen at the back of the porch.

At age thirteen, I had been hitting balls inside for well over a year. Eight-iron shots were my favorite—even plastic practice balls zipped off the clubface at an ideal trajectory. I loved the unique contour of that particular club, its braveness as it stood distinguished from the rest of the set. It had none of the angular assertiveness of the seven iron (which reminded me of a proud slice of pie), or even the bulbous, bloated roundness of the wedges. No, the eight iron, viewed at address, appeared to be exactly what it was: a jewel-like machine of measurement.

Over the past year, a small worn spot had begun to appear on the carpet, and while the blemish didn't please my mom, perhaps the thought that one day I would make millions on tour and buy her a dream house had made her overlook it.

My next swing, however, would prove a swipe no one could ignore. The backswing seemed ordinary enough, a decent little turn. And the transition was good too. Other kids had dogs; my swing was my faithful servant. The club dropped into the slot just as it was supposed to, and with a well-timed release I squared the blade forged from steel.

Next to my living room practice tee sat the family piano. Now a plastic practice golf ball yields a soft, light sensation when struck reminiscent of patting a balloon. On that fateful swing, I felt that little *whiff*, all right, which was followed by a most unexpected THUD. I had caught the side of the piano solidly with my eight iron, which had gone on to bury itself deep within the instrument's chamber, leaving only the silver shaft exposed. With my grip horrifically frozen in place, the image must have resembled a tableau in a French farce.

I didn't like to think of myself as a delinquent child. I was a good student, a good athlete. I ate my vegetables, didn't smoke, and felt compassion for kids less fortunate than I was. But knowing that I had done something wrong, I felt the criminal instinct take over.

Off I went on my bicycle to the candy store, then to the art supply shop across the street. I saw my mom's car parked in the supermarket lot and recalled her saying she was going to stop by her friend Phyllis's house after shopping. I figured I had an hour and a half to carry out my plan.

Back home I had no time to lose. I chewed a wad of gum and stuck it in the vertical "divot" slashed in the piano. Then, with the ecstatic freedom of Van Gogh, I painted the pink gum brown, hoping to match the hue of the instrument.

The end of this unfortunate escapade came swiftly. Mom walked in, groceries in hand, spotted the oozing gum dripping cheap watercolor paint on the side of the family treasure, and threw a fit. My dad, who on the golf course crooned over every great golf shot I hit like a tenor warbling "Sunny Boy" with a pint of Guinness in his hand, suddenly rejected the idea that golf encompassed spiritual values. My backside made the abrasion on the piano seem like the surface of a mountain lake at dawn.

The scar in the piano never healed, but mine did, and I grew up to be a golfer. My passion for the game has deepened and ripened and flashed hot and cold in a love affair that transcends the mere enjoyment of playing a game. Rather, it models the actual root of the word *passion*, based in the idea of suffering and the recognition that only from recognizing the pain of others can we develop compassion. Indeed, every time I play golf, as I see my own frustration mirrored in the exasperation of my playing partners, I remember what I learned when I was a kid swinging in the living room: The world is not a stage. It is a golf course.

Night Golf

I have heard many years of telling,
And many years should see some change.

The ball I threw while playing in the park
Has not yet hit the ground.

—Dylan Thomas, "Should Lanterns Shine"

The thwack of a golf club colliding with a ball is an out-of-place and dislocating sound in a suburban Long Island neighborhood, especially when heard in the middle of the night. Yet I forced my father to listen and respond to this peculiar percussion on more than one occasion back when I was a teenager growing up in Freeport along the Island's South Shore. I've already chronicled my exploits with swatting whiffle balls across my living room and the story of how one of these particular practice sessions ended with the clubhead of my eight iron embedded in the side of the family piano. So you would think a boy, even one as obsessed with golf as I was, would have learned the limitations of playing a game meant for the expansive outdoors inside the strictures of a modest split-level home.

And sure, I abided by such obviousness—for maybe three, possibly four, months after that. But then I saw a practice net advertised in the glossy pages of *Golf Digest* (little did I know or even fantasize that one day my articles would appear there!), and that net ignited my unlimited appetite for unfettered practice once again.

I confess that ads in golf magazines mesmerized me. They glowed with an absolute purity, the way Renaissance painters crafted halos glowing over the head of the Virgin Mary or other saints and angels in their canvases. I can still recall dreamily gazing at one such ad of a chestnut brown persimmon Kenneth Smith driver: it had a funny hosel, without any whipping or wrapping string, presaging both the ferruleless stainless steel hosels on PING irons and the bore-through hoseless drivers from Callaway still years in the future.

Even more compelling, perhaps leaning toward the fetishistic, were the pair of brown wing tip golf shoes I goggled at in those pages. What did those dots formed into a triangular pattern on the shoe's toes *mean*? I remember thinking to myself. Having never seen anything so handsome in my life, the shoes clearly stood as symbols of a nascent adult masculinity into which, as an adolescent boy, I was beginning to confidently stride. The odd thing is that I didn't really want the driver or the shoes at all. I just wanted to want them.

Yet I can honestly say that this practice net in *Golf Digest* all but called my name out as its rightful owner. In fact, I couldn't believe such a thing existed; it represented the perfect vehicle to transport my indoor practice requirements instantly out of the overcrowded living room (that damned piano ruined everything) and onto the back porch. I could set it up there and hit real golf balls into it. Those wimpy whiffle balls that felt like egg shells when I hit them and flew with the sickening fizzing sound of a wounded duck would become just a faint memory of a more primitive urge to hone my golf skills.

My dad said yes, he would buy the net for me. He probably would have gotten the wing tip shoes and the Kenneth Smith driver for me too. But, while I suspected owning things of such transcendent beauty would ruin them for me, a practice net with its airy imperfections not only seemed nonthreatening but required my love and attentive ownership.

The thing came in a big, broad cardboard box, which I ripped open like a predatory animal, hungry for improvement (anthropologists say sports in general arouse ancestral and archetypal memories of the hunt that still remain, however vestigially, in a human's genes).

I'm not sure whether the hitting mat of artificial grass came with the net or not—probably not, which meant it was an added expense for my poor old dad that, evidently, he incurred because hitting balls off the thin indoor-outdoor carpet that lined the cement floor of our porch would not have given me optimum feedback on the centered or oblique quality of my hits. If Ben Hogan could winter in the Palm Springs area just so he could practice on the great turf there, a little Long Island boy with dreams of dead-solid impact deserved a pathetic little patch of brittle, green golf ball mat.

Unfurled, the practice net stood before me like a majestic meshed silver screen, waiting to receive the projections of my golf game's hopes and fantasies in the form of nine-iron shots, five-iron shots, three-wood and driver shots, even chip and low-flying punch pitch shots, anything I wanted (save the high-flying soft lob shot) I could hit into the net, again with real golf balls!

Our screened porch sat a good five feet off the ground, and I imagined that perch as the elevated tee that majestically overlooks Carmel Bay bordering Northern California's Monterey Peninsula—the 18th tee at Pebble Beach Golf Links, perhaps the most hallowed hitting area in all the golf world. Even that storied plot of grass had nothing on my patch of carpeted concrete though. To complete the daydream, I even imagined the small artificial grass on my hitting mat as newly laid turf.

Little did I know that years later, while studying *The Golfing Machine*, I would read that Homer Kelley, its author, believed that a golfer could best improve his or her swing by hitting balls indoors into a net, because it eliminated the distracting obsession with ball flight that is inevitable when practicing outdoors. Of course, one could argue that a screened-in porch would qualify as being only *half* indoors. But even if my swing improved 50 percent, that would be better than harpooning my eight-iron into the side of the piano when hitting within the cocoon of my living room.

I can still hear the thunder of those first balls as I fired them into the net and feel my amazement at this simplest of gravity-defying devices as the net, while catching and dropping the ball, allowed me to finish the ball's flight in my imagination. In its muffled, cupped deflection of the ball's flying force, the net offered reassurance that anything on earth was possible. It said that all one needed to alter the forces of the universe, which seemingly rendered one helpless to shape one's own destiny, was a willingness to exercise—or build products that sprang from—the same kind of jerry-rigging imagination that had invented the net.

Thus a Flemish boy became a folk legend by sticking his finger into an Amsterdam dike. Ben Franklin hooked a key to a kite, and his discovery of electricity changed the outer world every bit as much as Moses or Buddha had transformed the human soul. In the annals of golf's spiritual evolution, this driving net belongs squarely (actually, rectangularly) in a similar category, because who, before its invention, could even *dream* of smashing full-blown golf shots while standing in a porch?

But that is exactly what I did—day and night—that summer back in 1969, the year my dad made that purchase on my game's behalf.

I lacked neither motivation nor opportunity to try some new swing technique out on—or, rather, *into*—the net. A tip in *Golf Digest* to "retain the angle" between the left arm and the clubshaft, for example, led to morning, evening, and even midnight net sessions, frustrating at first, as I tried to execute a five-iron swing with the wrists held back well into the downswing. Initially, this holding back had the paradoxical effect of making me release the club too early, which sent it driving steeply downward into the mat.

Shocks exploded up my arm and body from the cement floor under the mat. If I had been on an actual grass driving range (fat chance finding one of those at a public course on Long Island), I would have dug a hole deep enough into the ground in which to bury that net. However, as my wrists became more and more sore, my hold on the club loosened and softened, and as a result, lo! I found that such a supple grip was the key to retaining the angle!

The night in 1969 when the astronauts landed on the moon, I was sitting in front of the TV with a golf club in my hand. And wouldn't you know it! The first thing they did up there was play golf. Alan Shepard unfolded a collapsible six iron and struck the longest fairway bunker shot in history, with a perfectly timed, one-handed swing.

I thought that maybe practicing one hand at a time might benefit my motion too. After all, if a dude bundled up in the inflexible piping of a spacesuit could do it, for a seventeen-year old like me, with a normal range of motion and exceptional hand-eye coordination, a one-armed swing should have been a piece of cake.

My first attempt propelled the club—appropriately, I suppose—out of its normal orbit, and the ball, caressing against the hosel (of the six iron, of course), shanked at a dead right angle to the suddenly useless net. The ball ricocheted off of the house's wall, which formed the fourth side of the porch, and bounded around like a molecule shot with a laser in a physical chemist's experiment. The ball managed to touch every object in the room *except* the net and me, and how it didn't punch a hole in the porch's tall screens remains one of the great unsolved puzzles of my life.

But it's a good thing it didn't, because if it had it would certainly have evoked the specter of the eight iron–ripped piano in my dad's memory, and, if he didn't have me arrested right there on the spot, he certainly would have dismantled the net in front of me and chopped it into pieces small enough to burn in the den's fireplace. By some kind of lunar grace, though, I would live to practice my swing into that net for another morning, afternoon, and night.

Actually, that moon landing with its celestial sand shot began to exert an odd kind of golf gravity on me. More specifically, a somnambulistic trance began pulling me out of bed each night around midnight, when I would slip on some tennis shoes, unconsciously grab a club from my golf bag in my closet, and waltz down to the porch. Somehow my mom didn't seem to mind a half dozen or so golf balls perpetually lying on the floor of the porch, so my ammunition was always just waiting for me make a few wake-up swings before I started smacking one ball after another into the net.

I don't know the physics of it, but I suspect dark air conducts sound more efficiently than does air streamed with light, because the decibel level of my thwacking definitely approached deafening. Indeed, the oxymoron was anything but lost on my hard-working dad, as what to me sounded like the sweet music of dead-solid impact evidently vibrated with a more egregious buzzing in his ears, as if some newfangled alarm system signaling a danger previously uncategorized or even imagined rocked the entire house in warning. In other words, the sound of my hitting golf balls into the practice net on the porch woke my dad up.

Not one for theatrics, my dad expressed himself simply, clearly, and honestly. He also had a tremendous sense of humor, which he used to show affection for and trust in people. In fact, his use of humor worked as a kind of barometer; if he felt comfortable with a person he had just met, he would risk being funny with them right away. If he didn't trust a new acquaintance, he'd clam up and become as dour and indirect as a stockbroker trying to explain to his or her investor just why the market had dropped 247 points that day (not much humor there).

Well, obviously my dad knew me well and trusted me as much as any father can trust his teenage son, so a comfort level between us was a nonfactor in the ensuing exchange. He simply stood there in his long, straight, nondescript sleeping gown and, with his arm outstretched, at once rigid and confidently relaxed, said, "Give me the club."

He didn't even address me by name, which hurt my feelings a little bit. "Andy, give me the club," would have felt better. It might have taken a bit of the edge off of his demand and given it just the tiniest air of an empathetic request. But no, there was no room for negotiation, and maybe it was just too late at night (or early in the morning) for a more informal encounter.

So I gave him my club, which happened to be my four wood, the same Arnold Palmer laminated (or was it persimmon?) model that would forge a mirror of recognition between Amy Alcott and me as we hit balls on the same range at Pinehurst just a year later. There it went into my dad's sleepy paws, and it wasn't that I felt I would never see the club again—after all, my dad loved golf too and, as *I* was the one who had introduced him to the game, he would need me to have it back so we could go play together. It wasn't even that I felt guilty or punished—though I should have felt responsible for keeping my parents awake. It was that, even with my pajamas on, I felt completely *naked* without the club.

Years later I would read that the great jazz saxophonist John Coltrane had a horn in every room in his house so that wherever he was and whatever he was doing he could easily grab it and work on his fingering. There is also a neurological or psychiatric symptom called "hypergraphia," which manifests itself as the compulsive need to always write. I wondered why they didn't just call these people writers, as anyone who has ever written a book, as I'm doing right now, knows that the task feels limitless. You grab the pen and start writing, and you feel as if you will never stop.

My friend Anne Rice, the novelist, refers to this process as "essential dream," meaning that through a trancelike state, one merges with one's writing, as if one were simultaneously viewing and creating a dream in the very process of writing the words down.

Certainly someone like Vijay Singh, Tom Kite, Lee Trevino, Ben Hogan—name your favorite inveterate practice hound, golf ball beater, range rat type of personality, call them what you will—probably feels soothed, healed, and whole with a golf club in his or her hands. If that's the case, I'd have to put myself into their class or, I should say, *clinic* as well.

Where was I without my trusty four wood? Standing alone in the middle of the night in the middle of a screened-in porch in the middle of my youth, in the middle of the summer, with a useless driving range net staring me straight in my face and my father's oddly reassuring footsteps trudging up the steps, with my golf club in tow. Yes, where was I?

The next day, when I woke up and went downstairs to eat my cereal, to my astonishment (though not, ironically, to my surprise) the practice net lay packed away in its cardboard box, as if a newborn baby had crawled back into his or her mother's womb.

I obviously needed another way to satisfy the immediate urge—
indeed, the *need*—to work on my golf swing when and where I wanted.
Can you imagine John Coltrane sitting down to watch the evening
news without a saxophone?

That night, as I lay in my bed, clubless and netless, I realized that
the one thing I still had intact—and that had the capacity to work
with such perfect discretionary silence that even my father couldn't
take it away from me—was my *imagination*.

My confident and secure dreaming process succinctly reconstructed
in my restless mind's eye that eighteenth tee at Pebble Beach, which
overlooks the waters of Carmel Bay. It just so happens that my house
in Freeport stood on Bayview Avenue—get it? An avenue that overlooks the bay—and my street name too was no metaphorical figure
of speech, for there was an actual bay four or five blocks away!

My imagination formulated a plan instantly. All I had to do was
get on my bike, take a club, a tee, and a few golf balls, and ride down
to the bay. There a perfect little nameless beach awaited me, whose
grains of moist sand would certainly have packed themselves into a
smooth, flat, and firm surface not unlike—especially when experienced in the middle of the night—a golf course's tee box. More so,
because it too sat tangentially to the sea, I figured what I had there
was nothing less than a Long Island version of Pebble Beach.

Out from my house I flew on my bike, E.T.-like, through the neighborhood of modest houses to keep my tee time, about 3:18 a.m. on
that beach's first (and, I suppose, only) tee.

I would use a basic physics calculation to measure the quality of
my shots into the bay: the more time that elapsed between the click
of contact and the splash of the ball in the water, the longer my shot.
Certainly, determining the left or right curve of my shot would be
harder to do, but I didn't mind; I was willing to sacrifice a sense of
the accuracy of my drive as long as I felt certain of its (approximate)
distance. Remember, as recently as the night before, I had been able
to drive the ball only twelve feet or so forward before the net ab-
sorbed and annihilated the potential distance of my blow. In other

words, my interest in and connection with the great outdoors had been restored!

So I hit my shot. Of course I did. This story has to end someplace, even though I can't honestly say exactly how it did. Did the pause between the hit and the splash last long enough to satisfy me? I can't remember. Was the sensation in my hands at contact solid enough to quiet my body, mind, and soul? It's too long ago to recall. I do know this—that all of this really did happen, though its meaning beyond its being a tale of a young boy's passion for a game remains for me still, so to speak, up in the air.

Sam

People who know me know that I like to practice golf a lot. I may not be in the same class as Vijay Singh or Tom Kite when it comes to classic ball beaters, but for an amateur player who constantly sneaks away from his freelance keyboard in order to get to the driving range and hit four, five, even six hundred balls, I'm not altogether out of that league. Not long ago, after hitting my tenth bucket and feeling so sore I could hardly bend down to place another ball on a tee, I began to wonder if I was having any fun. And what, really, was the point of devoting an afternoon at a driving range if all I was doing was torturing myself? The more I found myself compulsively at the driving range, the more I began to sense that I was in the midst of an unbidden ritual and that the goal was to bring to my consciousness my rage for never really having tried to turn pro. Why didn't I? I had to ask that imaginary critic on my shoulder, the one in my head and my dreams, who, hovering over the dull, green, elongated plastic bins that held the driving range balls, kept telling me, "You're not good enough." It felt as if someone else were speaking those words to me—not me.

So I packed up my clubs, my back and wrist as sore as they had ever been, and headed for Starbucks. The plan was to sit down in front of my tall drip coffee and initiate in my notebook a kind of inner dialogue that would reveal the identity of the inner wisecracker whose authority seemed inseparable from his intentions of putting me down.

"Who are you?" And, "Come forth!" I furtively scribbled in my notebook between sips of scalding hot coffee and nibbles on a heavenly cool blueberry scone. But no figure emerged in my mind's eye for me to see.

"Tell me thy name!" I commanded, like a bad actor in a B-rated vampire film trying to free the demon from its occult prison by forcing it to confront its occluded human nature.

Hamlet, hearing the plea of his dead father, the king, imploring him to "Remember me!" couldn't have been as surprised as I when I heard blended among the smoky tones of Tony Bennett singing through Starbuck's sound system this muddied mesh of syllables struggle to say, "I'm Samsidhen."

I instantly separated this cryptic chord into the three strands that wove it, but to clarify how that sound only propelled the interrogation of my inner critic forward, I must tell the story of my father's three names.

It seems every male in my father's family was named Henry. I'm not sure why. Maybe the name's air of Englishness appealed to my dad's depression-era Eastern European immigrant parents. But there was a small problem, as my dad's mother wanted a Samuel, not a Henry. Too bad for her and too late too, because her brother (Henry, of course) ran down to the hospital the night my dad was born and named the newborn Henry. The "Henry"s didn't have the last word, at least, as my dad's mother raised her son as Sam anyway.

When a teenager, Dad got a job in a dry-cleaning store in Brooklyn. There were already two other Sams working there. The boss decided to call one Sam, another Sol, and my father Sid (I'm trying to tell this quickly so I can get back to golf). After that his friends called him Sid, and so did my mother, whom he met when he was eighteen, while everyone in his family, however begrudgingly, called him Sam.

That's two out of the three names. The third came with Sam/Sid's draft notice, which read, "Henry Brumer."

"Who's that?" my father asked his mother.

"You," she answered.

OK, after the war (*the* war, World War II), my father went into business for himself, and he probably thought, if "Henry" was a good enough name for the great *Uncle* Sam, then "Henry" it would be to all of his business and legal associates and friends.

So there you have it, the story of my dad and his three names.

And golf?

When my father was a kid, he never really considered golf a game for athletes. It wouldn't be fair to say that he characterized it as one for sissies, though everyone spouts that cliché. For Dad, handball, stickball, baseball, basketball, and football formed the constellation of his sports universe—that is, until I became interested in golf, which happened one day when I was twelve during a family vacation in Florida. That was where, by the pool at some hotel full of northerners, I met a kid named Bob Beckman from Toledo, Ohio.

"Hey, do you want to play golf today?" he asked me.

"What's golf?" I answered.

I knew, of course, what golf was, but even then I liked to exercise my deadpan sense of humor. In fact, knowing what the game of golf was literally didn't mean I comprehended its essence. So when I said, "What's golf?" I wasn't being funny. I was being truthful, and the truth is never in and of itself funny, not without something a little wacky or out of whack layered over it.

Well, Bob was a little country club boy, a Davis Love the third in miniature, who pronounced his vowels with a quick high-pitched midwestern twang, rather than D. L. III's more luxurious, albeit subtle southern drawl. Bob Beckman had blond hair and tanned skin and wore a perfect polo shirt and had a very good swing.

For me, though, "swinging" meant baseball. On the diamond, I had a great eye, an uncanny capacity to get the bat on the ball. My friend Pete's mom swooned over my swing at Little League games. Maybe because I couldn't see myself swing, I didn't understand her enthusiasm. My own sport passions were to change, though, the moment I teed up that golf ball with Bob Beckman on the first hole of that Florida golf course, whose name now I couldn't remember for a million dollars. Of course I played with rented clubs, though it's surprising to think that in 1965, they had rentals to fit a thirteen-year-old boy.

I swung at the golf ball as if it were a baseball, and I met the rubber cover of that balata the way a wrecking ball finds the broad wall of an old and useless building. But instead of tumbling down, the ball took off from me in a tight, parabolic arc. Later, not much later, I would appreciate the shot as a slight "draw," that slight right-to-left curve that looked unlike any baseball flight I had ever seen. In fact, the ball seemed to slow down in midair, a result of its long flight, and as it "drew," it seemed to elongate into a preternatural profile.

That was the objective description. The subjective was different. The great Ben Hogan, so reticent that Ben Crenshaw described him as a "sphinx," once made a TV commercial to promote his golf club company's forged irons. There, the "Wee Icemon," as the Scots called him, declared that the feeling of a well-struck shot "traveled up the shaft, through your arms, and into your heart." Indeed, I too felt my first shot, not in my heart, but as a setting off of a spasm that seemed to start in my loins and freeze my entire body in a paroxysm of pleasure.

That night I returned to the hotel, and in my room, for no apparent reason, I began to write poetry. I experienced the impulse as something cosmic, nonintellectual, full of grace and easy motion. Art itself had entered my soul via that beginner's luck golf shot. Later, I would find a fascinating arcane link between golf and poetry. It turns out that the very word for poetry, *verse*, is short for *reverse*, referring to the plow's turn at the end of each straight row it cuts on the farm's field. Poets, too, write and organize their words in lines, which, reversing themselves as they reach their ends, establish the feeling and flow the poet wants. A somewhat warped, silly or distorted for my purpose syllogism would state: poems are written in lines; farms are plowed in straight rows; golf courses are nothing but plowed fields; golf courses are poems.

So I had become a golfer, a man, and a poet in one fell strike that day I first played golf with Bob Beckman in Miami. Soon, though, all I wanted to do was play golf or go to the driving range. Since I was only thirteen years old, I had no way to get there, which is when and where Sam enters the picture. Notice I didn't say Henry or Sid. No, Sam the family man—my dad, not the businessman or free-spirited youth—was the one who stepped forward to take me to play and practice golf.

As I got better at golf (and I progressed quickly—by age sixteen I was shooting par on the Black course at Bethpage State Park), Sam decided to take up golf himself. It seems, in fact, that he waited just long enough to allow me to get good enough at it so that I could teach him how to play. Such role reversals were common in my family, perhaps in all families. So there I was, a son teaching a father how to play golf, which got Dad to take me to the course. Sure, I valued the time we spent together on the links. At least that sounds like the right thing to say. Yet, dang it, any real golfer knows that playing the game actually obliterates the entire world around you, or annihilates you vis-à-vis the world. So there you are as you play, one with the universe but also the odd man out of it ideally dissolved of ego and appetite.

My dad wasn't very good at golf, which surprised me because he had been such a terrific athlete as a kid. But he was forty years old when I was twelve, and while I was no more gifted athletically than he had been when he was my age, golf had come to me naturally, the way water rises up to hold a duck. For Dad, the only thing "ducky" about his game was what golfers on adjacent fairways had to do when his shots sprayed every which way but straight.

Early on, then, I found myself facing the Oedipal dilemma of a son about to outdo his father, without even suspecting that some fathers don't relinquish their superiority without a pretty good fight (or that victory for the son often comes with a price tag of inner conflict and guilt).

I lived for playing with my dad at Bethpage. On weekends, we'd get up at 3:30 a.m. and arrive at the sign-up window at 4:30. In those days, they had a simple sign with removable numbers next to each course's name to tell you the length of the wait. We'd see: "Red course, 2 hour 30 minute wait; Green course, 2 hour 45 minute wait; Yellow course, 3 hour wait," and then, "Black course, 25 minute wait." People feared the Black course for its difficulty, but for me, choosing it was a no-brainer. We'd sign up for the Black more times than not, tee off near 7 a.m., and be home at noon. It just seemed like a golf course to me, certainly a very beautiful one, and one on which I had to learn to hit the ball very straight. Clearly, the experience spoiled me, because I thought this was how all golf courses were supposed to be. I haven't played there in close to thirty years now, and with the changes and variations they made to the course for the 2002 U.S. Open—changes that made some of the best players in the world cry uncle at its feet—I'm not sure I want to go back there again. Some things bring more satisfaction in memory.

Playing the Black taught me another lesson, one as unexpected as it may sound odd. You see, after walking the Black course (Bethpage didn't have golf carts in those day on any of its courses, and today, while you can ride the others, you still have to walk the Black) and returning home, I would lie on my bed and fall fast asleep. Before drifting off, I remember saying to myself, "This is what people mean when they talk about being exhausted." Previously, the idea of being so tired during the day that one needed to go to sleep seemed thoroughly foreign to me.

Back on the driving range as an adult, when I just couldn't get the clubface squarely against the ball, and as I began to curse and berate myself with names too shameful even to print, I'd always soon hear the name "Sam" rise again from the depths of my unconscious.

It was Dad, of course.

But what, really, was Sam criticizing me for? What had I done wrong in his eyes? I could think of nothing. Was it a "sin" to be ambitious, to have a goal, to dream the dream of wanting to be a pro someday? I remember an NPR segment I had heard years ago about cocaine addiction. It said that the feeling cocaine induced in the brain was the same one people felt when they looked forward to something pleasurable.

"Holy mackerel!" I remember thinking to myself. "The *American dream itself* is the drug!"

My father feared failure the way some people fear heights. He just didn't want to go there, and the fear was based in his depression-era upbringing. I'm sure he vowed many times that should the opportunity for prosperity call, he'd answer, follow it, and not look back. As a soldier in World War II, he had fought as many others did to liberate Europe and to save the world from Hitler. Failure was no option there either. While extremely intelligent, Dad never gravitated toward school and he knew, without having to struggle internally, his vocation. Certain that he didn't want to work for someone else, he went into business for himself. Like great athletic champions, successful businesspeople, and maybe all other types of geniuses, he could simply block the thought of failure out of his mind. When I told him, later, that I wanted to be a poet, he said, "Write greeting cards."

Didn't he understand that one could fail at doing that too?

I remember playing golf one day as a kid with my dad and a couple of men, strangers, with whom we were teamed to make a foursome. Impressed with my ball-striking skills, these gentlemen lavishly showered me with praise. But rather than allow me to soak in such building blocks of healthy ego formation, my dad said, "When he practices and hits a bad shot, he throws his club on the ground and shouts, 'There is no God!'"

I never said that. I threw clubs, yes, and often (many fathers punish their sons for doing so, but how many realize their sons are throwing the clubs, symbolically at least, at them!), but I never blamed my frustration on God. My dad, in his contorted quasi-masochistic manner, I realized much later, was trying to *protect* me from failure, even though it didn't frighten me in the least. Had I finished my literary studies (or been a more intellectually precocious youth), I might have quoted Nobel Prize–winning writer Samuel Beckett's commandment to "fail better," for what began to paralyze me as adolescence segued into young adulthood was the fear of trying.

Then, like so many questions, problems, and seemingly impossible conundrums whose solutions come ready-made when your mind is distracted and you least expect it, my complex relationship with my dad and golf simply resolved itself through the following dream.

First, my sister Karen tees off, with a beautiful little power-fade drive of about 210 yards down the fairway that comes to rest in perfect position on a par four, dream hole fairway. She's just short of a little pot fairway dream bunker. I'm impressed, and not only does it surprise me that she had this shot in her bag or repertoire, but I find it curious that she swung at the ball right-handed. You see, Karen can never figure out from which side to swing when she hits balls on the range (and in real life, she has never played one round of golf).

I'm up next in this dream round, and I poke a three wood that starts on the same line and at the same height as my sister's shot, and I think, "Darn, can't I hit the ball farther than Karen? What does this part of my dream mean?"

But, thankfully, I see the ball land about where hers has stopped and then watch it roll and roll some more, and this relaxes me into the dream's machismo sensation of superiority. If in dreams we become captive spectators of our own souls' movies, in real life we're just the productions' overworked actors, too tired and busy to understand the meaning of the scripts we're enacting.

But in my dream the ball I hit gracefully takes the full left curve of the fairway and, rolling rollickingly, finally comes to rest in the back corner of another fairway bunker.

So that's the dream. And where was Sam during this whole episode? Nowhere! That's the point. That name, the one signifying family, with all of its obstacles, the one that emerged on the range to say that I'd never make it, never made an appearance! Rather, it was my sister Karen who served as my unexpected guide, as if she had dressed up as Virgil to my Dante and we were heading out into same Halloween night we used to trick-or-treat on together as kids.

And what we saw together in the blurred brilliance of imagination's scrim that caught and wove life and dream together into the single magical fabric was that things rarely work out perfectly in golf or in life. And what we learned was that rather than seeking the unambiguous fantasy of safety or perfection, it was more fun to just follow the ball along any and all fairways. Because like the old bouncing balls atop the words of those cartoon songs we loved as kids, life always gathers itself, then slides forward with a slender grace to the next syllable, sound, and word, where it pauses, rests, puffs out its chest, and then bounds ahead once again.

That's my story, my song and poem, and the fact that in the dream the ball ended in a bunker seems now a thing quite different from failure. Rather, it simply predicts and points to another dream or round of golf to come, where I know that I will be able to figure out the exact shot I want to play next.

Girls and Golf in Pinehurst

I wasn't thinking about girls when I accepted my mother's generous invitation to lend me her Mercury Cougar to drive from our Freeport, Long Island, home to Pinehurst in North Carolina to play some golf. I was thinking about golf. Perhaps I should have been thinking about college, too, because it was the summer of 1970 and in September I'd be enrolling at Rutgers University in New Brunswick, New Jersey, for my freshman year. Indeed, though this was just two years shy of the publication of Michael Murphy's mystical novel of education, *Golf in the Kingdom*, I never really considered how golf could function as a life teacher or even how it might truly be a metaphor for life. It was a sport for me, a game I loved, and I wanted to go to Pinehurst to sharpen my skills to make the Rutgers University golf team.

Not only was I not thinking about girls, I wasn't even thinking about what subject I would major in at school. All I was thinking about was golf.

Fredrick Law Olmsted, the architect of New York City's Central Park, also designed the town of Pinehurst as a replica of a New England or northeastern town to make the vacationing Yankees comfortable. Indeed, he succeeded, as the place looked anything but unfamiliar to me as I drove into the crescent-shaped gravel driveway of the Pinehurst Lodge. However, while there is no driving range to be seen when walking through Central Park, I had fantasized about the range at the resort from the moment I entered the Washington DC metropolitan area on my drive south.

Nor was I disappointed when I got there. The range at Pinehurst was indeed a thing of beauty, with an expansive, manicured, horseshoe-shaped hitting area and a tree-lined landing zone that framed the space with unobtrusive grace and southern insouciance. Here was

a zone of free focus exempt from the consequences of the good shot/
bad shot dialectic that defines the anti-range, the golf course itself.

When you practice, you are supposed to have some specific goal
in mind, and mine that day had to do with keeping my head back
behind the ball through the impact zone with my long irons so I
could get a little more loft on the ball with those clubs. It turned out
that keeping my head back had a different benefit as well, for it wid-
ened my peripheral vision considerably (and raised my prospects,
as it would turn out), though taking in what's tangential to the target normally offers little benefit to golfers, who do their best to elim-
inate any and all distractions.

But this turned out to be anything but a normal practice session for me, as just down the practice tee to the left there was a very
pretty young girl hitting balls. I took immediate notice of her blond
hair, blue eyes, and a figure the likes of which I figured I'd encounter soon enough at college. But how this body swayed! It took my
breath away.

Ben Hogan is said to have hit shots as if they were fired from a cannon, with the ball coming off his clubface with a distinctive sound
at once crisp, authoritative, clean, and terrifying. He hit the ball so
hard that it produced an immediate extended echo, "BANG BANG!"
like that, as if he had hit one ball twice. His fellow pros would stop
their practicing on the range during a tournament not only to watch
him hit balls but to listen to him do it as well. I'm not going to lie and
say this girl's capacity to produce Hoganesque acoustics was what
turned my eighteen-year old head that day (and my fifty-three-year-
old memory today), because she didn't apply enough force into the
golf ball to do it. But her presence set off some sort of fireworks in
my soul just the same.

Rather, her swings produced polite, sincere, and slightly muffled
"clicks," which were well-practiced and serious sounds just the same.
In fact, her music repeated itself with a skilled consistency as each
click vibrated in the same sweet register as the one preceding it. Her
swing slung mid-iron shots off her clubface in perfect parabolas. In
short, this girl could play!

Peripheral vision works both ways, left and right, and out of the corner of my other eye, I noticed another feminine shade swatting balls with the same degree of proficiency and nubile style.

Then another, and another, and another, all equally attractive and all striking down and through the turf with fearless Diana-like downward blows. I felt as if I had died and gone to heaven, as there I was, the only young man in the center of a golf universe of girls, all preparing, as it turned out, for the USGA girls national junior championship at Pinehurst that week.

Not only were these kids great golfers, they were also friendly! It was a great relief that week not to have to ask each girl I met there, "What's your major?"

I knew their major, golf, just as they knew. So to their select sorority of what seemed like a hundred girls, champions or near champions from every state in the country, they admitted me as a fraternity house of one. Though I felt like a boy again, and acted like a boy with my flirtatious giddiness, I used my recently departed boy status to gain the confidence of these girls' parents, who, to a girl, accompanied them on this exciting and important trip.

A college man! Now there is someone you can trust!

The resort didn't prohibit its regular guests from using the practice range that week, so I found myself hitting golf balls alongside the girls, some of whom would become Hall of Fame golfers in the years to come. I noticed during one such session that Amy Alcott and I were using the exact same model of irons and woods—Arnold Palmers.

Years later, after I had moved to Southern California and began writing about golf, I saw Amy at an LPGA tournament, though this time I had to use my media badge to gain access to the range. Since it was a Thursday, the day before the competition would start, I felt reasonably comfortable interrupting Amy's practice to introduce myself. Amy was well on her way into the Hall of Fame at this juncture in her career, and she had met a lot of different people along the way. Even so, I confess to feeling a bit disappointed (and embarrassed) when I asked if she remembered meeting me at Pinehurst that end-of-summer week in 1970.

"I'm sorry. I've met a lot of people," she said politely. I appreciated her tact in not blurting out for my fellow golf writers on the range to hear, "Of course, I remember that week very well, but I don't have the faintest recollection of ever having met you there or anyplace else." Then I re-created the scene on the driving range at Pinehurst, where we hit balls and talked together for well over an hour. "And we were both playing Arnold Palmer woods and irons," I said, "Do you remember those jet black persimmon woods with the bright red acrylic face inserts?"

That last morsel of detail gave her pause, and as she broke from her practice session she looked me squarely in the eye with an expression of depth, puzzlement, and curious recognition that struck me as the outward correlative of déjà vu's interior gaze.

She said, "You're right. Those were the clubs I played with then."

I evidently made a greater impression on Margie Leno, a swarthy, pretty, brilliant, and magnetic girl who was also the girls' junior golf champion from Wisconsin. Our discussion while hitting balls quickly broke the boundaries of golf and spilled into talk about our hometowns, our parents and siblings, my imminent freshman year at college, and her hopes of attending a top university herself in a couple of years. I felt I had met a true soulmate, and the newness and excitement of seeing myself reflected in another with such specifically articulated detail elevated the already exotic atmosphere at Pinehurst that week into an even more complete paradise. We became friends, and rather than watch her carry her own golf bag during the competition, I offered to caddy for her.

Now an eighteen-year-old young man has a lot of energy, so I didn't think twice about playing golf or practicing on the range in the mornings or afternoons and caddying for Margie during her matches. That was, however, a lot of walking, and my feet ache now just thinking about it.

Anyway, I clearly had other vocational callings besides caddying awaiting me, as I couldn't keep her clubs in their correct slots in the bag. I also misread her putts and almost broke a couple of rules on different occasions, which—had Margie not been the brilliant, Stanford-bound young lady that she was so that she literally stopped me in my tracks from completing these offenses—would have gotten her disqualified from the tournament. As it turned out, she survived my best intentions to help and made it to the event's semifinals (or maybe it was the finals) against Laura Baugh, who wound up winning the whole thing.

Laura presently works as a tournament analyst on the Golf Channel, offering subtle insights into the psychology of today's top players. But back then she was golf's version of Anna Kournikova, a beautiful young woman with a lot of sex appeal. Sponsors would snap her up the moment she turned pro—she would become particularly popular as a bikini-clad, pin-up calendar girl—but this was her week to shine as a golfer.

Unfortunately, all the girls knew too well of Laura's potential commercial cache, which was already being discussed regularly in wider golf circles. Frankly, many of the kids were envious of Laura, and the collective cold shoulder they gave her only turned icier after she won the tournament.

I found Laura crying alone shortly after the awards ceremony near the bag rack by the cart shed, the petty rejection by her peers obfuscating her joy in winning this prestigious national title. The fairy tale of my week at Pinehurst ended at that moment, and I stood there stunned at the unfamiliar avuncular and empathic feelings I experienced as I did my best to comfort Laura. It seems I had crossed some conceptual yet very concrete emotional line in my life, and without consciously trying I had become an adult.

I'd like to think that, were I to run into Laura Baugh today, as I did Amy Alcott years back, she would, indeed, remember meeting me at Pinehurst.

As for Margie Leno, she changed her name to Jamie Zimron, left golf for a while, became a world-class, competitive black belt aikido champion, then returned to golf as a teaching pro based in Southern California who uses martial arts philosophy and technique as the physical and spiritual center of her golf lessons. She's probably giving the golf ball one hell of a Zen-like karate whack these days, but I'll never forget her jet black ponytail rebounding gently against her shoulders as she swung on Pinehurst's driving range as if the very soul of midnight graced and deepened the bright playfulness of the day.

Little did I know that our meeting would affect my life in such a circuitous fashion as it ultimately did.

I would eventually transfer colleges after my second year at Rutgers and complete my education at the University of Wisconsin in Madison. Margie and I remained in touch, and she arranged for me to meet a friend of hers there whose sister and her husband were publishers of poetry books in Berkeley, California. I met these two during one break or another in classes while they were visiting Madison; then, shortly after graduating college, I looked them up when I found myself living in Berkeley, not playing golf but writing a lot of poetry.

They had just published a book of poems by the since-deceased Stan Rice, and they invited me to the book publishing party at their house. I would eventually study creative writing with Stan in graduate school at San Francisco State University. Stan's wife, the novelist Anne Rice, helped me get started in freelance writing, and through the Rices I met many visual artists. All of this led to my fanning my work into three streams: art writing, golf writing, and creative writing. My hope is that these rivers will merge in this book, *The Poetics of Golf*, and I'm doing all I can to keep their tributaries open enough for them to do so. But I never realized until writing this piece that I could trace their singular source to the practice tee that fateful week at Pinehurst during the summer of 1970.

Golfless in Berkeley

Approaching Berkeley

In Berkeley during the 1960s and 1970s (and maybe even now), golf was a four-letter word. Of course, in Berkeley, being the anarchistic capital of the rebellious spirit that it is, four-letter words are required vocabulary for admission. But *poet* is also a four-letter word, and, as they say, if you throw a stone in Berkeley (skull a wedge shot?), you'll hit a poet.

"Let's all get together and be individuals." That's always been the city's implicit mantra, though its commitment to self-expression seems to exclude playing golf as an acceptable genre. This seems to me peculiarly ironic considering that Michael Murphy's office lies right across San Francisco Bay in Sausalito, and we all know Michael now as the author of golf's spiritual bible, *Golf in the Kingdom*.

In the song "Devils and Dust," Bruce Springsteen sings, "Fear's a terrible thing / It will turn your heart black, you can trust . . ."

But if fear can darken and sicken the heart, shame can annihilate it.

I can't say that Berkeley made me ashamed that I loved golf, but the truth is, while I lived there through most of my twenties, that's exactly how I felt about the game. Basically, I didn't play.

My songwriter and guitarist friend Robby Krieger, of the Doors, told me that in his band's heyday during the late 1960s, he too couldn't let others know that he loved golf. He didn't use the word *shame* to describe his feelings, but he said that if he wanted to get in a round while touring with the Doors he would have to sneak away to play. Actually, JFK did the same thing, because although he loved golf, his spinners thought that were his love to become public, people would associate him with Dwight D. Eisenhower, a proud golfer if ever there was one—and Kennedy's political opposite. It all goes back to the clichéd and ridiculous notion that only rich, right-wing Republicans play golf, and leftist-leaning souls or artists or anyone even marginally outside of the corporate box would have to play the game under cover.

Yet, today, heavy rocker Alice Cooper, country-and-western star Willie Nelson, Christian/pop singer Amy Grant, national universal health care coverage advocate and former president Bill Clinton, and countless other unusual suspects have come out of golf's very deep closet to play the game openly, in many cases more times a week than your dentist, stockbroker, army general, evangelical minister, drug company sales rep, and small appliance manufacturer put together. It seems that even Bob Dylan has picked up the sticks (see "Bob'n Around" later in this book).

Every year Tiger Woods has a rock concert in Las Vegas called Tiger Jam to benefit his Tiger Woods Foundation. Who do you think he asked to perform at the event this year—Perry Como? It was Sting.

Yet our souls grow only through sacrifice that requires us to give up something that we think we need in order to gain something even more useful, and therefore, meaningful, though we don't at first know what it is. The gods love sacrifice. Doesn't all life flow as a gift from some single source, and doesn't it stand to reason that that fountainhead periodically needs replenishing?

On the biological level we're all nothing more than recyclable goods. We're fast food quickly preparing ourselves as nutritious meals for worms and flowers, who keep busy day and night preparing to give themselves back to us and the larger gastronomical engine of the earth.

So giving up golf for a while in Berkeley doesn't sound or feel as shameful anymore as it would have if, say, God required me to quit playing the game and I didn't. Besides, if the feeding of my golf game to the hungry universe meant in the big balance sheet of energy exchange my tiny immaterial psyche would find itself spoon-fed with the manna of art, well, that seems like as good a gamble as throwing horses over a cliff as a means of procuring sunlight.

I stopped playing—hard to believe as it is that the gods, or God, would have cared. I'm not the first person to struggle with naming God. The ancient Israelites wouldn't allow themselves even to say the name; instead they said "Yahweh," which roughly translated means, "I am that I am." Let's forget that Popeye the Sailor Man said almost the same thing about himself—"I am what I am and that's all that I am." Yahweh is pure being and meaning in and of itself, and not something pointing to another thing to derive its meaning. "Is is is" is closer to Yahweh's essence, as far as I can tell.

Yet what in the world could God do with golf, and why would God want golf as the raw material to alchemize into art for me?

Of course I dare not presume to think I know what God thinks—it's bloody hard enough to know what I think—but something the poet Robert Bly said to me as I interviewed him for the Berkeley poetry publication *Poetry Flash* speaks to—if not answers—this question perfectly. He said, "With competition, no feeling can come in."

Bly's cryptic, semishorthand way of speaking reveals his reserved and reticent Minnesota (by way of Norway) family roots. His magic as a poet lies in his capacity to compose such clinky syllables into fluid and sagacious words of meaning—that is, poetry—not unlike the way the keyboard compositions of Thelonius Monk rattle ordinariness into elegance. I knew what Bly meant: the athlete in me had to sacrifice his competitiveness in order for art and literature to integrate feeling back into my life.

That said, I couldn't help but think of Bobby Jones, whom some consider the greatest golfer ever and who gave up the game in 1930 after winning all of its major tournaments, because competition drove him to the brink of a nervous breakdown.

Jones, not known to speak in parables, said that there was "golf and golf" (which sounds curiously similar to the sacred tautology, "I am that I am"). He meant that golf had two manifestations: competitive and recreational. He had obviously had enough of the first variety, which is why he founded the Augusta Golf Club as a place where he could enjoy the second with his friends. That it quickly became the home of the Masters tournament, which no one in his or her right mind can dismiss as a noncompetitive event, seems a paradox to me. Maybe once a competitor, always a competitor. Having fulfilled his ambitions for competition, Jones never factored seriously in the event; perhaps he decided to play recreational golf during the Masters while the others played competitively.

"This game will put you in a straitjacket," my old friend the sadly departed Dave Marr once told me. It certainly wrapped its sleeves and buttons pretty tightly around Bobby Jones to the extent that he had to build perhaps the most beautiful golf course in the world as his personal playground to free his soul from competition's deadening vice.

"Golfers weren't meant to stand over a putt for a million dollars," Marr continued. "They were meant to play in the presence of people whose company they enjoyed in beautiful surroundings."

That's not much of an endorsement of how they do it on the PGA Tour. Perhaps the Tour should change its slogan from "These Guys Are Good" to "These Guys Are Nervous Wrecks."

I remember feeling stopped in my tracks when I heard Bly's comment because it snapped into perspective my whole struggle with golf: on the one hand I couldn't extinguish an inner competitive fire to "beat" the game, to play it perfectly, yet as a human being what did I really value in life? It was not batting a little white ball around; it was my feelings for and those I received from other people and my daily effort to feel some sense of intimacy with nature, both of which combine to form the stuff of art.

But wait a minute. Aren't artists as crazy and obsessed as golfers? I think some are and some aren't, but I believe firmly that art itself in its conscious and skillful composing of conflicting forces (be they visual in the plastic arts or linguistic in fiction, drama, and poetry) represents a life raft of mental health and an opportunity for personal redemption.

Therefore, my involvement in the arts in Berkeley greatly enriched my life so that now I'm able to play golf soulfully, not solemnly, and can humbly search for the game's ever expanding bouquet of meanings, not brutishly break my neck pounding range balls while trying to master an activity that has proven itself essentially unconquerable.

But what can we say about the nature of sacrifice in general? Why does it work so powerfully, and why have we become so unconscious of its role in our everyday lives?

For the ancient Greeks sacrifice functioned the way working out does today for young business executives—the pain leads to the gain kind of thing—and it played as much a part of everyday life as the businessperson's rote stopping in at Starbucks for a nonfat grande decaf mocha (with no whipped cream). For example, the Greeks believed that the god Helios pulled the sun across the sky in a horse-drawn chariot, and they strode to the top of cliffs overlooking the ocean and threw carriages and horses down into the water, believing that thus Helios would get the vehicles he needed to carry out his daily task.

Yet a sacrifice isn't exactly a contract or a trade: "I give you a chariot and a horse, and you give me sunlight every day." It's more like a prayer or a wish for what during the 1960s we called "good karma," as in "One good deed deserves another," behind which lies the blind faith that in the Big Picture, this is what fair play is really all about: "I just gave you your horse and carriage; don't you think we deserve a little sunshine in return?" That sort of thing.

I'm thinking out loud about all of this because I'm still wondering just what God or the gods might do with my offering of my golf game?

They would take it and play golf with it, of course, and be grateful for the little bit of recreation and fun it has to offer. Can't we picture the universe as a huge golf course and the galaxy as a driving range? What else do those meteors and shooting stars and comets and dust particles all buzzing playfully around in random crisscrossing patterns at different heights resemble but balls hit at a crowded multi-tiered practice facility?

By deduction, then, I see that what I needed returned to me by the gods of art and writing who rule Berkeley was a more playful attitude toward life and, by extension, toward golf.

Art is "pure and intense play," penned Antonio Machado, Spain's greatest poet of the twentieth century. "There is no one more intense than a child at play," wrote the German existentialist philosopher Nietzsche (he obviously didn't witness those rather serious ancient Greeks tossing the horse and chariot over the cliff).

Life in Berkeley

Carl Jung, the Swiss psychoanalyst, believed that the desire for perfection belied or hid a fear of ambivalence, which becomes meaningful for golfers in the context of a famous line by Ben Hogan to the effect that "golf is a game of misses."

In other words, as a game of *imperfection*, golf frightens as much as it frustrates perfectionists, which is partly why I found so soothing and reassuring the question that the young lady working at the café, seeing me come in with a book of poetry, asked me: "Do you write poems?"

I told her, "I try, but I'm not very good at it," to which she replied, "But in art you can't be wrong whatever you do."

Oh, if only golf could be like that. In fact, translated into golfese, the equivalent sentiment would posit, "In golf whatever you do is wrong." Why? Because golf is a game of misses.

That young lady in the café had it right—while I might write bad poetry, I couldn't by definition write *wrong* poetry, and I like how this feels very much.

Even so, while not playing golf in Berkeley, the computer in my golfer's mainframe kept constantly matching incoming data on art and literature with stored information already there about golf, and it stored these new couplings away in brand-new files. Of course, I didn't know this was happening at all as I was just immersed (and, as it turns out, distracted) in a very dynamic and stimulating period of my life.

What's more, being young, very young, my mind thought in unsophisticated binary dynamics, much like a computer: "I'm an artist; I can't also be a golfer."

The thought that I was both—or even the more difficult notion, neither (meaning that a person's identity transcends his or her interests and vocation, that is, that I was—Popeye and God notwithstanding—"who I was" and not what I did)—represented a degree of consciousness that even Berkeley didn't give me.

Indeed, the artists and writers I met in Berkeley thoroughly intoxicated me; it all felt like a dream, a Dionysian journey through rivers of pure wine, and it seems odd that in the context of writing about golf I'm for the first time publicly acknowledging some of them.

The first person I want to thank is novelist Anne Rice, whom I met the first week I arrived in town in 1975. Anne and her late husband, the poet and painter Stan Rice, were friends of relatives of a college classmate of mine at the University of Wisconsin, who brokered the introduction.

Anne and I hit it off immediately thanks to our initial conversation about Shakespeare's play *Othello*. I claimed that the drama's villain Iago, intent on deceiving the warrior Othello into a murderous jealous rage over his wife, Desdemona, not only mirrored Brutus's schemes to derail Popeye's romance with Olive Oyl but also stood for the destructive potential of the human ego (Anne was kind enough not to remind me that Freud wouldn't "invent" the concept of the ego for something like three hundred years after Shakespeare's death). She liked my ideas and responded to them with brilliant ones of her own. Her intelligence, kindness, humor, and that most rare virtue of all, capacity to listen to others, impressed me to no end.

When I asked her what she did, she said that she had just finished writing a novel about vampires, and to my follow-up question about who was publishing it, she said, "No one has accepted the manuscript yet—everyone's rejected it so far."

Herein lies lesson number one, because two weeks later Knopf gave Anne what amounted to at the time the biggest advance ever for a first novel. Not only was *Interview with the Vampire* a huge success, but it launched Anne's amazingly prolific career, Dickensian in its blend of popular appeal and artistic purity, which, with her best-selling last novel, *Christ the Lord*, has not taken its pedal off the metal for one New York publishing second ever since.

The lesson Anne's example taught me was to never give up trust in your talents and dreams. "Trust instinct to the end, though you cannot render any reason," is one of Gary Player's Ten Commandments of Life, all ten of which I had the pleasure of working on with him (he elaborated on each commandment's relevance to golf and life, and I developed them into an article) for *Gentlemen's Quarterly*'s South African edition.

In golf we have to trust our own inner conception of the swing, even if it goes against the teaching gurus' proclamation about what's stylistically orthodox or correct. Comedian Flip Wilson's wonderful female persona/character named Josephine, which he created on his 1960s TV show, used to say, "What you see is what you get." In golf it's more a matter of "What you get is what you see," because our internal visualization of our swing and shot for the most part determines its outcome.

Dave Stockton, one of golf's all-time great putters and a multiple major championship winner, once said that "golf is 90% mental," before catching himself and modifying it to "100% mental." So much for the new Tiger Woods–influenced golf workout mania in the gym!

We also have to trust our instinct to play with the equipment that performs best for us, even if new clubs with supposedly "better" technology supposedly render our gear outdated and inferior. As in quantum mechanics, the many paths our lives present become our singular truth only when a "wave of reality" collapses potential possibility into eventual experience.

Descartes said, "I think therefore I am." In the Jewish faith, the *intentions* of our thoughts are what God ultimately reads in our minds and uses to judge us. In the film *Field of Dreams*, the family built the baseball field, and they came. Retired Supreme Court justice Sandra

Day O'Connor had a pillow in her office with the phrase "Not always right, but never uncertain" embroidered on it. In other words, so-called popular wisdom has always valued and endorsed the power of positive thinking, only now we call it quantum this, that, or the other thing. In golf we must settle into an intense belief state regarding every aspect of our game and let all ambivalence crumble away into fearless unreality (Freudian or otherwise).

I learned a different but ultimately more profound lesson about golf via literature from Anne's husband, Stan Rice, who was my poetry-writing professor in graduate school at San Francisco State University. During one lecture on verse Stan paused for a second, looked off into art's interminable distance, and then, as if in a trance, declared, "When you get right down to it, the essence of poetry is nonverbal."

I remember feeling like I was about to fall off the chair when I heard that. If poetry is essentially nonverbal, what was I doing studying how to write here in graduate school?

I came to understand that Stan meant poetry uses words to release in its readers or listeners a pure quality of feeling that, ironically, can't be put into words—that is, that when we read or hear a good poem, we experience *feeling*, not language.

I've mulled over Stan's idea recently out on the golf course, especially during periods when I happen to be playing well, because in the midst of those rounds I'd get the very distinct feeling that the essence of playing golf is nonverbal as well. Certainly, playing the game involves thinking, but it seems like a kind of thinking that doesn't depend on words to formulate thoughts. More so, thinking in words while playing golf somehow clouds or annihilates the thoughts themselves.

Say I have a 155-yard shot to the green, for which I'd use a seven iron. Rather than think in words, "Seven iron for a 155-yard shot," I find myself looking into my golf bag for a club with the visual cue "7" engraved on the club's sole.

Next, how do I hit the ball with this silent "7" iron to the hole? By thinking the myriad of verbal thoughts and cues that I've learned comprise the story of a golf swing from the setup to its finish? That doesn't sound like a nonverbal method of playing the game to me. Rather, I would instinctively generate enough force from my body to the club to the ball to propel it to where I want it to go—to the flag. It isn't a matter of using fewer word keys to get this process going; it comes down to successfully turning off the verbal part of the brain completely and solving the problem at hand with the aid of other kinds of thinking skills. Thus Charlie Chaplin or some other silent-era film star would be the ideal archetype of a golf teacher, because he would have to give lessons silently.

Modern dance legend Martha Graham called her school "the house of pelvic truth." The brain thinks in words, but the pelvis thinks in movement, as do golfers.

When Fred Couples says, "When I'm playing well, I don't even aim," he means that he doesn't aim in words, such as *right, left, high,* or *low.*

They say Ben Hogan refused to tell his supposed secret of his superior ball striking because he didn't want to give his competitors the same advantage it gave him (or because he was miserly by nature). I think he didn't tell anyone his secret because he couldn't, since he didn't experience it in words.

If poetry and art and golf aren't about words, what *are* they about?

My closest artist friend in Berkeley is the metal sculptor Joseph Slusky, who says, "Making art for me is about the magic of being alive today; whatever went wrong yesterday, we have the now in which to dance."

It's that one-shot-at-a-time attitude that roots us so salubriously to the present. "What shank?" fired Jack Nicklaus famously back to a room full of reporters who asked him what went wrong on that squirrelly, low lateral laser he lost dead right off the tee at a par three hole during a U.S. Open. "The past is behind you / Let nothing remind you," sang the Four Tops.

Similarly, when friends asked the late poet William Stafford how he managed to honor his commitment to himself to write poetry every day when surely there were days when he didn't feel well or inspired or interested in writing, Stafford simply answered, "On those days I just lower my standards."

Now, when I find myself not playing golf well, I remember these words, and all that art and poetry taught me about golf and life during my marvelous and all-too-short tenure in Berkeley. When I asked my sister Karen, a beginner at golf, what was it she wanted from golf (see "What Do Golfers Want?" later in this book), she answered simply, "To hit the ball."

After playing the game all these years, and having studied the swing in books and from the game's top golf instructors with the fervor of Yeats's "bald-headed" scholars, I haven't reduced my standards to Karen's yet. However, the next time I find myself riddled by mysterious pull hooks off the tee, bladed iron shots that fizzle into the air's mocking nothingness like a punctured balloon, chili-dipped chips with no ameliorating salsa in sight, and yipped short putts from six feet that finish sixteen feet from the cup, I may well give it a try.

Pure Wine

I moved to Memphis, Tennessee, from New York City in 1986, the year my mother died. I had been in a long-distance relationship with Adelaida, a college professor who lived and worked in Memphis, and we felt it was time for us to live together. My sister and I had cared for our dying mom in New York, where we grew up, and I never had any other thought or feeling about doing it other than that I would. After my mother was gone, though, there was no longer a reason for me to stay in New York. So that's how I arrived in Memphis, mourning the passing of my mom while joyful in the presence of my beloved.

But I can't say that Memphis and I mixed so well at first. I had been teaching English as a second language at Hunter College and writing a lot of poetry, book reviews, and art criticism in New York. My dad and I played a little golf, and when we did, I used his second set of clubs while my clubs, the ones I had played with on my college golf team, remained in my friend's attic in Berkeley, where I had lived for eight years after graduating from the University of Wisconsin. In Berkeley, too, I played golf sporadically, not much, really, as at that point in my life the game had receded in importance for me.

In fact, since I've mentioned college golf, I'll point out that although I did compete for two years on the Rutgers University golf team, it was academic considerations, and not the game, that led me to transfer to the University of Wisconsin in Madison. Suffice it to say that I woke up one day with a lot of blisters on my hands from swatting balls and not a lot of thoughts in my head about Shakespeare or Ezra Pound or James Joyce or Virginia Woolf, and I was an English major! When it dawned on me that I had the rest of my life to play golf but only two short years left to be a college student,

I decided to transfer to a school that I didn't associate with golf at all: the University of Wisconsin.

I was Stan Freydas, an artist and a longtime family friend, who encouraged me to consider Madison as a place to finish my undergraduate studies (his daughter, May, had gone to school there). But that's not really relevant to the story I've started to tell. The point is that, by 1986, when I moved to Memphis, golf was becoming less important to me than ever before. Now I wonder whether my passion for the game was hibernating, frozen in protective amber during Madison's cold winters, springs, and falls (not to mention a good part of its summers).

I did find an old eight iron in a second-hand store in Madison and bought it for two dollars, and I managed to get my hands somehow on a couple of whiffle golf balls, which I would hit across the empty basement of the rooming house in which I lived. You can place a golfer in the middle of a Wisconsin winter, but you can't take golf out of someone who has tasted its eternal summer—or so my subterranean eight-iron actions had proven to me.

So jump forward a good twelve years. There I was in Memphis, ready to begin what seemed like the start of my truly adult life, signaled and sanctified, I hoped, by a loving, committed relationship to another human being.

The problem was that I found myself with very little to do there. On one hand this was ok, because I was still grieving the death of my mom and I was able to live comfortably for a while on a small insurance policy she had left me as well as by my half of the sale of her beachside condominium in Long Beach on Long Island. Anyway, Memphis seemed like the land of leisure. It *sounded* like that to me, too, because the region's lingua franca offered slow, rolling syllables that I savored like the lapping sounds of its venerable old man, the Mississippi River.

Let me give you an example, though I'm aware that such diversions drift me farther away from my subject of golf.

We were in a Mexican restaurant called Ay Caramba overlooking the river, where I felt peculiarly pleased with my new home's cultural diversity, though I was experiencing it in a touristy eating establishment replete with black velvet paintings of conquistadors hanging next to one kind of Elvis memorabilia or another. The place was mobbed. Sipping my margarita with Adelaida, I heard my name booming over the cocktail lounge's loudspeaker. The hostess was calling us to our table.

At least I thought she was calling my name, because here's what it sounded like to me: "Aundy."

No. That's not quite it.

Rather, it was more like "AiYuAundeee," a slur of such dexterity that in my mind it instantly became a metaphor of my new home's ability to draw out any and all experience to its full and elongated limit. It was a metaphor of southern leisureliness.

So there wasn't a tremendous amount of pressure from the outside or from the inside on me to find something constructive to do. Shucks, it seemed as if it took them twenty seconds to say my name. So what was the hurry?

My easing into the slow South took the form of sitting in the new cafés I had quickly scouted out, writing poetry each and every day. My favorite café was La Baguette, oddly situated with a trace of southern or French charm among a row of shops that lined a huge concrete parking lot. And wouldn't you know it, my drive to La Baguette took me right past a public golf course called Galloway, or was it Audubon? Whatever the name, its greens and fairways whistled with either the distant allure of Ireland or the simple sounds of birds.

I kept eyeing it as I drove past, its lovely old elm and dogwood trees beginning to turn colors in late September with the slow and reserved politeness of southern gentry (as opposed to the fiery rebelliousness of New England's woods). And I could swear that the more I looked at the course, the more the course looked back at me.

Straining my neck as I drove by in my Honda to watch a player or two hit off of the first tee, I felt that the game was calling me back home, though I sensed the irony, too, that somehow my mother's death had paved the way for this reunion.

If the little café where I sat alone and daydreamed my poems into being represented a safe throne of creativity, Galloway Golf Course (let's agree to call it that) stood as a massive temple of worship, a redemptive open-aired Vatican within which I might integrate my disparate demons—the golf I loved as a boy, the love of nature that sparked my interest in art, and my efforts to write poetry with the articulated rhythm of the body making a dynamic golf swing. Maybe I also sensed that walking the links again might connect me to a community of new friends, as one never plays alone, at least not for too long anyway.

Standing on that first tee the very next day aroused strikingly similar feelings as those of the very first time I had played on a golf course, way back when I was twelve years old in Florida. It must have been the set of rented clubs I used on both occasions that established the déjà vu, and I thought of my old clubs, those Arnold Palmer blades and persimmon woods buried in my friend's attic in Berkeley, and wondered if I'd ever see them again. What really melded the past and the present—married them, I might say—was the click and feel of ball on club off the tee on number one at Galloway. Suddenly I knew that this almost forgotten sensation had grafted me to the game, again at least until death would us part.

I was back, involved again with my people, the golfers, and integrated with and inseparable from my surroundings, the golf course, though the true sign that I had staked out my space in the community came when the young people working at my newly adopted driving range began to give me free golf balls to hit.

It could have been a form of pity, actually, when these young workers, most of whom weren't even into playing golf, began to shower those golf balls on me. I was hitting many, many buckets a day. Yet there also must have been some kind of recognition of the passion with which I approached practice, because if they thought I was merely *obsessed*, I doubt that they would have sponsored my ball pounding so wholly and warmheartedly. Probably they would have recoiled in distrust, without making engaging eye contact with me, without smiling or initiating a conversation; but in fact they did smile and talk a lot to me soon after I started showing up at the range day after day after day.

One overweight girl with tender blue-dyed hair, torn black Converse sneakers, and a lip ring (how divergent in style are those who work the registers at driving ranges from those at country club pro shops) once even surprised me with a question.

"Do you believe in *bi-u-ig* clothes?" she asked, referring to the fact that the flat posterior I inherited from my father made my pants drape loosely around my thighs and droop sloppily from my hips. "Because most men I see your age believe in *tight* clothes, and you wear big and *loose* clothes and I really admire that!"

One rarely enjoys such an honest if not raw exchange while buying (or in this case *not* buying) a bucket of balls at a driving range. The vulnerable, lost tremor in that young woman's voice made me want to adopt her on the spot and take her home to Adelaida, where the combined tolerance of our natures would provide a sufficiently nurturing environment for this lass so that she might turn her life around, feel loved, and, blue hair or not, become somebody.

Instead, I just did my best muffled chuckle in the affirmative to let that young driving range attendant know that I felt that she and I were riding in the same unstable boat in the turbulent seas of life, sartorial styles, and driving ranges.

It was also a good strategy to keep the flow of free golf balls coming, and while I wasn't proud to be a golf ball freeloader, I had to do what I had to do in order to sculpt my swing into perfection.

So there on the outskirts of Memphis, I found myself free to hit as many golf balls as often as I wanted, because the attendants were giving me buckets for free. My swing, more than my soul, would be the beneficiary of this fancily finagled arrangement.

They say that practice makes perfect. What I found was that practice made me a *perfectionist*.

One day, after my fifth or sixth or seventh bucket of balls, I noticed a portly yet shadowy figure standing behind me watching me practice. I've long known that hitting golf balls this way had a hypnotic effect on me, settling my psyche into an oceanic, trancelike condition of bliss, but what I hadn't considered was that *watching someone else* repeatedly strike shots in this manner could induce such a state in others.

When I say portly and shadowy, I'm thinking of a blend between Alfred Hitchcock and Martin Scorsese: an Anglican, massive coolness animated by an angular Latin darkness. That I remember him as a mix of two movie directors isn't coincidental. After all, what I'm remembering centers completely around the act of looking: me looking at the ball, this man looking at me, the reader looking at these words (I suppose I'm trying to look at my readers right now too), all of us figuring in our collective mind's eye the motion picture of my golf swing.

"Pure wine," the Maestro (that's what I came to call him) said. Or at least that's what I thought I heard him say.

"Pure wine." He said it again, as I struck one solid seven iron after another into the air above the barren, hard brown ground of the driving range.

Now I sensed that the libation to which my not-so-secret admirer was referring had to do with my swings and the shots they produced; they were good swings, I suppose, producing *good shots*—and I understood that the Maestro experienced both the swings and the shots as some form of intoxication.

I remember turning toward him in acknowledgment.

"Thanks," I said softly but also a bit perfunctorily, because I didn't want to interrupt my practice. "Thanks a lot."

"Pure wine," he repeated again, but this time it was more to acknowledge my having acknowledged his compliment.

We never played golf together—I guess you can say we practiced together—yet to this day I still can't rationally figure out just what the words "pure wine" really mean. I regret not having asked the Maestro to explain that phrase, not so that I could bask a little longer in the ambrosia of his praise but to again deepen my understanding of how metaphors join two disparate images together and ferment a totally new, transcendent thing into existence. Golf.

"Pure wine."

Whatever it meant or means or doesn't mean, it still sounds good to me.

Cheating at Golf

The woman I've lived with for twenty years, although a loving and attentive spouse, has taken no interest in the game of golf. As for Adelaida's interest in *my* interest—nay, my *passion*—for golf, well, this has posed a kind of ontological dilemma for us.

What do I mean by an "ontological dilemma"? The definition of ontology has to do with the problem of being and the essence of objects (such as me, Adelaida, and the game of golf) and their relationships (such as me to Adelaida to the game of golf and vice versa).

The act of *being* in a *relationship*, it seems to me, finds its essence in the back-and-forth process of interacting, like electricity zigzagging powerfully between two poles. If an individual thinks and therefore *is*, then two people interact and therefore *are together*. This is no groundbreaking definition of a relationship. In fact, it's pretty much the standard one.

So, if golf has been such a big part of me, how can Adelaida relate to me without relating to golf? That's the ontological situation in a nutshell.

Let's just say she has tried (she took one swipe at the driving range once and serenaded the ball with a gentle whiff of pure air like an eagle's wing lazily flapping past a mountain's cliff). We'll leave it at that. On second thought, if we were to leave if at that, I'd have to leave this at this, but the ontological boat has to sail on just a little longer over love's stormy sea before I reach the shore of my topic: cheating at golf.

Adelaida experienced—that is to say, felt—my focus on golf as something exterior to our relationship, as a kind of cheating on her, which is why from time to time she would refer to the game as "stupid golf." Now I recognize the cliché here of the golf widow, but that implies that the game has killed the husband and that he will never return, not to mention the elements of grief and mourning such an absence creates in the widow. I don't think one can find a symbolic morsel of any of this in the phrase "stupid golf." Anyway, reading that Ben Hogan referred to golf as "a fickle mistress" legitimized the nugget of romantic infidelity inherent in the sport for me.

Our nuptial détente erupted into war on the day of the 1994 Northridge earthquake here in the Los Angeles area, where Adelaida and I live.

While the intense shake, rattle, and roll of the event alarmed me—indeed, scared the heck out of me—as much as it did anyone, once the vibrations abated and it became clear that because the freeway between my house and the office in which I was working had partially collapsed, I realized that I wouldn't have to go to work that day and I decided that I would use this unexpected day off to play a round of golf.

Sure, I understood that the earthquake had unnerved Adelaida, but I figured the worst was over—that just as lightning doesn't strike in the same place twice, the earth's geologic pressure wouldn't trace a new fissure right on top of the one it had just drawn on the ground. Nature, I reasoned, was a far more original artist than that. Clearly, the worst had come and gone, I said to myself. At least that was my story that day, and I stuck to it long enough to drag my clubs out of the house and into the trunk of the car. While a good deal of chaos, confusion, and fear gripped greater LA that day, the sky itself grew clearer and calmer in an ironically reassuring way. I suspect not too many others shook themselves as thoroughly free as I did from their domestic and vocational duties and allowed a kind of anarchic golfer's instinct to take over and drift them to the course.

Golf infidelity morphed instantly into total betrayal in Adelaida's mind. But a golf bigamist, by definition, must divide his affections between the animate intimacies of human love and the inanimate droolings over a game.

That was long ago. Looking back, I regret my actions that day. Notice I didn't say "decision." At that point I was as incapable of con-

trolling my urge to go to the golf course as the earth was of refrain-
ing to explode.

One would think that my "earthquake round" would have established its own permanent fissure between me and my golf and Adelaida. But she's a kind and generous woman, so eventually she for-
gave my beeline sprint to the first tee when the quake signaled my
day off, much like a gun's firing sets athletes off their blocks to start
a race.

Yet the scars of marital faithlessness remain long after the way-
wardness that caused them has passed. And with those ridges of hardened memories, a couple never really regains the same kind of bliss-
ful footing in each other's affections that they enjoyed before.

It is not only sexual betrayal that breaks the previously unblem-
ished surface of love's calm lake, for as soon as one rod in the bipo-
lar dynamic of a relationship leans far enough away from its compelling albeit opposite charge, it drifts untethered back into its own
private interests again. Then all that stands between the essential
barrenness of our existential space and a regaining of love's harmo-
nizing garden is to leap over this border, break down this wall, and
muster up enough courage and will power to take an interest in your
significant other's interests.

So imagine my shock when, while we were at the lovely Ojai Valley Inn just south of Santa Barbara for a little weekend getaway, Adelaida said she'd like to come along with me during my round of golf.
Stunned, I accepted her invitation. Why not? This would be the new
start both of us had wanted, the Cold War of golf's détente, a renewed
dance of courtship, where my booming drives, crisp iron shots and
dead-centered putting would reveal to her again the steely harmony
of masculine nerves and muscles of which I was made.

It rained like mad Friday night, and there was a question as to
whether the director of golf would even open the course for play
Saturday morning. He did, but he wouldn't allow motorized carts
on it because of its waterlogged condition. This inspired many resort guests to cancel their rounds and opt for the more relaxing lu-

brications of the spa's native California herb medicinal rub. Who wouldn't better enjoy the moisture of a steam room, or even the sweats of the sauna, to slopping around over soaked grass with a golf bag (designed to fit against the back of a golf cart) slung over one's shoulders or lugging a rusty pull cart with spindly legs through pools and puddles?

I happened to have a lightweight carry bag, albeit one with a wicked kickstand. The left leg swung out violently when I picked it up, engaging my own right leg in a kind of duel of man and machine. If I hadn't owned such a bag, I probably wouldn't have wanted to play that day either.

My drive off the first tee split the middle of the soggy fairway, a good enough shot to impress anyone with even an inkling of golf knowledge. But, alas, Adelaida had none.

So down we descended along the slippery slope of the elevated first tee, like Virgil leading Dante into a mazed version of golf Hades, where only the wisdom of an experienced guide can enlighten the novice about the dangerous depths of human foibles and sins.

But, who was leading whom? Certainly, Adelaida could teach me nothing about golf, or so I thought. Nor could I teach her about the sport, because up to this point she had lacked even the most rudimentary nugget of curiosity about the game, and interest must precede learning.

My next shot didn't soar or sail as true as my first. In fact, the ball kind of clunked and chunked its way well short of the green, a victim of the soaked fairways, which caused me to strike it fat. I knew I could do better than that, and I thought the wet conditions required me to pick the ball more cleanly off the turf rather than drive the iron head down and through it. All I needed to do was to keep my head elevated nice and level through impact, and the low point of my swing would rise correctly and accordingly in response to catch the ball first, cleanly, in its rear end.

So I reached into my pocket, grasped a second ball, and dropped it on the ground.

Now if the Northridge earthquake had created havoc throughout all of Southern California, the little physics of my placing that second ball on the ground set off a seismic explosion in Adelaida on the scale of the Big Bang.

Actually, it wasn't the act of tossing the little pellet on the grass that moved this narrative forward but, rather the fact that I hit that ball, solidly as it turned out, right on the green.

In other words, it was this enactment of the word *mulligan* that triggered an automatic response in Adelaida, and, like one either hypnotized or unself-consciously breaking the rules in a game of charades, she screamed forth a passionate "You cheated!"

So surprised was I to hear this phrase, which echoed through the air as if uttered within the depths of a rocky canyon, that I turned completely around in a 360-degree search to find the source of its utterance.

If she had not shouted it again, and again, and again, and again— "You cheated, you cheated, you cheated, you cheated!"—I might have dismissed it as a figment of my imagination (since I honestly believed Adelaida's ignorance of golf was so categorical that she didn't know hitting two balls broke the rules), as in an hallucinatory indictment of some druid that protected the woods lining these fairways, with nothing better to do than shame unsuspecting golfers even though they might not be out to set the course record or post an official score in the tournament but just wanted a little fresh air and exercise in beautiful surroundings.

However, I've never totally dismissed one of their kind as the source of what felt like an inappropriate, not to mention harsh, reprimand.

2

Lives of the Golfers

What Do Golfers Want?

Golf and desire go hand in hand as snugly as a flagpole sits inside of its cup. And, like that flexible target, what golfers want from the game one moment sways, bends, and becomes ruffed and unclear only to snap into clarity and calmness a moment later. Passion ignites flames of both joy and despair. After all, golf is a "fickle mistress," as Ben Hogan called her (and Hogan was the steadiest soul with perhaps the most repeating swing the game has ever known!). Therefore, at any given moment, the game can shine on any golfer with benevolent grace or hostile animus, without seeming compelled to offer any rhyme, reason, cause, or word of warning for her vicious vicissitudes.

Buddhists say that the purpose of their lives of long devotion to meditation and study is "to be able to eat when hungry and sleep when tired." So knowing what one wants isn't the easiest of human challenges or tasks.

"The Wife of Bath's Tale," in Geoffrey Chaucer's classic *The Canterbury Tales*, tells of a young man sentenced to death for violating a maiden in a field. The Queen, though, decides to give the lad a chance to save his skin. If, in a year's time, the boy can answer one question correctly, she will spare his life.

The question was, "What do women want?"

Well, the fellow wandered the land for a year but by execution day hadn't found the right answer. While he was sitting dejectedly along the side of the road, an old woman, deformed with illness and age, approached him and said, "I know the answer, but if I tell it to you in return you have to promise to grant me a wish."

What more was there to lose, the young man thought, so he agreed.

"What women want," the elder said, "is power over men."

That was the right answer, and the Queen pardoned the young man.

As he was getting ready to go out drinking with his friends, the old woman appeared and said, "My one wish is that you marry me."

His buds went out to the pubs alone, as the young man realized that he must keep his promise. But don't think he felt overjoyed about it. He looked so darn sad that the old lady took pity on him.

"Well, here's the deal," she said, realizing that now was the time to let him know that she wasn't any ordinary mortal woman but a creature with supernatural powers.

"You have a choice. You can marry me the way I am and I'll always love you and take care of you and you never have to be jealous, obviously, or to worry about your so-called buddies hitting on me all the time. Or I can change myself into a beautiful young woman your age and you will indeed worry about that a lot."

It seems the boy was a fast learner.

"You decide," he answered, thinking that the notion of women exercising power over men had done him one good turn already that day. Since he gave her the option, the old woman turned herself into a young beauty *and also* vowed to be loyal and faithful to him for the rest of their days. This cheered the kid up considerably.

So I figure there is something profound at the heart of the game of golf, too, that golfers want, though they may not know what that is or even that they are indeed longing for something that the game hasn't yet given to them.

As I accumulated responses from golfers of all different skill levels and involvement with the game, I found a heartwarming glimpse into people's souls, and often a degree of golf-oriented introspection and vulnerability, that surprised me.

I'll start with what I want.

Andy Brumer (that's me): I want to know my swing.

Bobby Clampett (my friend, PGA Tour pro, and CBS Sports golf commentator): I want to compete and win, and I want the relationships I make through golf to enrich my life.

Karen Brumer (my sister, and a beginning golfer): I want to hit the ball.

Lindsey (a young woman working in the pro shop where I practice): I want lower scores. [Among all the golfers I questioned, she was the only one who said she wanted this.]

Cameron (a young man working in the pro shop): I want a consistent swing, so that one minute I don't think I have it all figured out and then the next day I'm completely at a loss as to how to swing.

John Monteleone (my literary agent): I want each course I play to be intelligently designed with interesting holes throughout.

Mr. Wong (my friend, age midsixties): At my age I want to get out there and have a good time and exercise. I don't expect a good game because I don't have one. I just ignore the bad shots. They're out of my mind the moment I hit them, which wasn't the case when I was a seven handicap and practicing all the time. I don't even keep score anymore; I just enjoy the game.

Leanne Wong (my friend, former Junior World Champion and scholarship golfer at the University of Southern California): I want people to expect less from me as a golfer now. I don't play much because I'm a working mom, but people remember me as a good golfer, so they expect I'll play well. I played the red tees the other day with some women golfer friends, and it was so much less stressful and more fun. That's it: what I want is to play the red tees! Oh yeah—I also want people to stop asking me to give them lessons.

Cary Schoen (teaching professional, mini-tour player, aspiring PGA Tour player): I want to be able to make a living playing golf. ["Yes," I interrupted, "but that's a professional goal. What is there deep down as a golfer that you want to experience in your heart about the heart of the game?"] I see. What I want is a reliable swing—so that I can use it to make a living playing golf.

Todd Yoshitake (head pro, Riviera Country Club, Pacific Palisades, California): I want the perfect shot. Every time I step up to the ball,

PART TWO

I want to imagine the perfect shot, visualize the perfect shot, feel the perfect shot, hit the perfect shot, taste the perfect shot, hear the perfect shot, then see the shot turn out perfectly.

Mike Chwasky (editor, *Golf Tips Magazine*): There are two things I want. First, having fun playing golf means hitting solid shots most of the time. It's just not much fun when you don't. Next, I love to spend a day outdoors on a beautiful course. The best is when the two go together, as they did for me when I was lucky enough to play the Old Course at St. Andrews. I was hitting the ball well, it was a beautiful day, and the course was fantastic.

Gregg McHatton (PGA teaching professional): I want to know what I'm doing with my swing and be able to repeat it.

None of these responses, however, seems to answer the question "What do golfers want?" Sure, they speak to what each person wants individually, but they don't speak of what golfers collectively desire. After all, many women responded to the young man's question by expressing their personal wants and needs as women, but the Queen sought one answer that encompassed what *all women wanted*.

Sure, some people may say, "That's why we want something, because we don't have it," just as women in Chaucer's fourteenth-century England wanted power over men because they didn't feel they had any. But I just can't help thinking that there's a common denominator to what golfers desire, and *my* golfers' wants as they expressed them to me didn't represent a collective, uniform base.

It occurred to me that, clearly, the young man made out pretty well in the "Wife of Bath's Tale," winding up with a wife both beautiful and true by *willingly giving up his power* to the old woman. My golf teacher Gregg McHatton says that women swing the club better than men do because "they are more in compliance with the forces of physics than are men. The men are strong enough to override these forces, but that just means they are better 'steerers' of the ball"; they try to willfully muscle the ball straight, whereas many women swing more freely and naturally and willfully *give up* their attempt to control their swings. In short, they dance in tune with nature's gravitational field as it correctly *pulls* them through impact.

The late Mike Austin, Guinness Book of World Records holder for the longest drive in competition (515 yards), used to say that women's large and strong hip physiology makes them better suited anatomically to swing the golf club correctly than are men.

Robby Krieger, my musician/golfer friend, often tries to kill the ball, and after he hits it way off line, he'll turn to me and ask, "What did I do wrong?"

"You swung too hard," I tell him every time he asks.

"Yes, I know, but what did I do *wrong*?"

In other words, swinging too hard doesn't register as a bona fide error in Robby's mind, or in the minds of many men. Yet Annika Sorenstam, whose swing and length off the tee most amateur male golfers would die for, seems *incapable* of swinging too hard!

And yet every single time Robby drops and plays a second ball after miss-hitting a drive because of swinging too hard, he hits a *dead-solid perfect drive* that goes a mile! Everyone says that happens because he (and all of us who experience this vexing frustration) has taken the pressure off of himself, and that's completely right: he has taken the pressure off of himself to hit the ball too hard because he knows that, since he can't play his second shot, how far he hits becomes inconsequential.

Many men distrust the saying "swing easy," but they would jump on the bandwagon if they understood the science behind the cliché. Through the impact zone, the hands function like a pulley. The smaller this pulley, the slower the hands move but the faster the club travels. Look at slow-motion video or high-speed swing sequence photographs of such great players as Tiger Woods, Sergio Garcia, or Ben Hogan (or anyone with a truly dynamic golf swing), and you will see that they drive their hands well forward toward the ball during the downswing. In so doing they create a very small pulley that whips the golf club at tremendous speed into the ball through the impact interval. The faster the club swings, the farther it hits the ball.

The opposite is also true: the larger the hands' pulley, the more effort golfers need to generate clubhead speed, and excessive effort tends to dissipate, rather than create, power. So it's not just folklore that says that a slower (hands) swing hits the ball farther.

Sam Snead understood this intuitively when he spoke of "the 80 percent solution" as a key to his length off the tee. He meant that he swung the driver with only 80 percent of his power.

I think Sam did give himself over to a more feminine principle of swinging with rhythm and feeling, with sensitivity to the timing of his hips pulling his shoulders through impact, keeping his feet rooted and planted to the chthonic earth, which allowed him to produce more power with less exertion.

So Sam gained power by giving up some of his power, just as the young man in the "Wife of Bath's Tale" got what he wanted by sacrificing some of his power to the old woman.

Now I'm critical in general of the way a place like Los Angeles worships human youth and beauty, but I think these can be very good things in a golf swing. What golfer wouldn't want an effortless, unforced swing that unfolds in harmony with the earth's gravitational forces? That such a stress-free swing results in longer, straighter shots and a healthier body seems reason enough for any guy to give such a swing governed by the feminine principle a downright manly try.

Pro-trait #1: Arnold Palmer

Here's a king but not of people or land. Rather, his domain encompasses the limitless expanse of human frustration: golf. That's why when he gets ready to hit his driver, he kind of grimaces at the ball sideways, as if unsure about wanting to hit it. Or is he preprocessing the degree of disappointment a poorly struck shot will bring, or practicing to sufficiently calm the ecstasy that solid contact sings? The word *sufficiently* is the key, because what Palmer counsels us on through his appearances on TV is that doing our best is always good enough. For that he wears a crown studded with the jeweled endorsements of motor oil, wrist watches, dry-cleaning stores, and a mad myriad of other products and services that, with his name attached to them, become odd accouterments of golf. Don't we all have to drive the golf course on a tractor, the way Arnie does to promote his oil? And eating Wheaties out of a Palmer box will keep our heads steady when we swing, right? His well-named whirlybird finish bespeaks his skills as a pilot—for the skies may feel like paradise to a man whose life is striking down through the turf.

Once, long ago, I interviewed him, though he kind of balked and barked and tried to blow me off. His trusted agent, "Doc," had set it up, so I felt comfortable holding the King to his commitment. I kept thinking of Arnie's wife, who in interviews would say her husband "treats everyone the same, from presidents to bellhops." So naturally I was expecting the warmth and unconditional acceptance I never got from my father! But what Mr. Palmer said was, "Who did you say you were again?" He did the interview though, and when I expressed couched anger over how he greeted me by saying that his trademark umbrella "has had its share of ups and downs over the years," he just laughed with that broad, uninhibited grin that made me look to see if the TV cameras were nearby again. "He's a King all right, " I thought, because he's flawed like all people. It made me a little teary, inexplicably hungry for Wheaties, and wanting to fill my Honda up with Pennzoil, whether it needed it or not.

Light My Fivewood

"If the doors of perception were cleansed everything would appear to man as it is, infinite."

—William Blake

"Right now, I'm working on eliminating a reverse pivot that I only seem to make with my driver."

—Robby Krieger

It is 1965, and a group of talented musicians attending UCLA are about to form the Doors, one of America's most original and influential rock groups of the 1960s. The group's lead vocalist, the poet and visionary Jim Morrison, and keyboardist Ray Manzarek had met as students at UCLA's film school. Drummer John Densmore and guitarist Robby Krieger took a Transcendental Meditation workshop together. Krieger, then nineteen years old, had already been playing golf for ten years. A shared passion in their search for the "infinite" through music brought these four young men together.

Krieger was even then passionate about golf, as unlikely as that must have seemed to his bandmates. "I started playing golf at nine or ten when my father joined Riviera in 1956," the soft-spoken and thoughtful Krieger, now sixty, told me as we sat in a golf cart waiting to tee off on Riviera's third hole. A sharp dogleg right, the hole flows toward a set of the course's signature deep and dramatic greenside bunkers, which frame the green like storm-driven ocean waves.

"The course looks pretty much the same now as it did then," Krieger said, "but it cost only $600 to join back then." Corporate memberships at this shrine of American golf today go for considerably more.

I spoke to Todd Yoshitake, Riviera's director of golf, about Robby's game. Yoshitake said that he swings the club "like he plays the guitar, smooth and fluidly and with rhythm." I liked that, and I found Todd's analysis of Robby's overall game even more engaging: "His mannerisms on the course are like his music; a little complicated, a little dark at times, and really interesting. With a guitar in his hand, Robby's a maestro. I think he's looking to achieve that same kind of mastery in his golf game."

Move over, Shivas Irons!

The glamour, buzz, and crazy energy of touring with the Doors didn't allow Krieger much time to work on his game.

"I kind of gave golf up for about twenty-five years, though even with the Doors, I'd still play maybe once every two months," he recalled with a slightly wistful sense of loss in his voice. Of course, a lot of overworked teaching pros would practice their scales until their fingers bled to get to play golf that regularly. But did the image of himself as a golfer *and* a member of the Doors trouble him? "I didn't worry about that stuff," Krieger muttered.

Robby says he started playing regularly again about fifteen years ago when several of his musician friends in LA took up the game.

"I thought, 'Well, I might not be very good, but I know I can beat these guys,'" Krieger recalled. It didn't take long before, in his own words, he became "addicted" to golf again.

"Just the other day I was thinking about how the only thing I like to do in my life is play: play golf and play the guitar. Now, is this a worthwhile way to live? I think it is, because golf, like music, is really an art form.

"When you think about it," he continued, "to get a little ball this big from five hundred yards away into a little hole in four or five shots is pretty impossible. And the only way you can do it is by overcoming your self, and that kind of pushing away at the barriers of your limitations is what art is all about. It's like Zen—you bring something up from deep within."

Krieger continues to explore the depths of himself and his art with his Robby Krieger Band, and he also continues to perform the Doors' music with Manzarek and other musicians. Krieger writes much of the material for his band, and that should surprise no one. After all, he penned both the music and the lyrics for several of the Doors' megahits, including "Light My Fire," "Love Me Two Times," "Touch Me," "Love Her Madly," and "Spanish Caravan," among others.

It may be, however, that Krieger's celebrity is a bit wasted on some of today's young.

"I know Fluff Cowan, who was Tiger's and Peter Jacobsen's former caddy and Jim Furyk's present one," Krieger said, fighting to repress a smile. "And a few years back now, Fluff introduced me to Tiger: 'Tiger, this is Robby Krieger, who was the lead guitarist for the Doors,' Fluff said. Fluff told him that Tiger later asked, 'What's the doors?'"

Tiger's friend and former basketball great Charles Barkley calls Tiger a "nerd," and Robby would no doubt love hearing this.

What about the late and legendary Jim Morrison? Does Robby think that had he lived he might have gotten into playing golf?

"Absolutely not," said Krieger. "Jim was more the 'lounge lizard' type than the golfer type." With that, we headed over to Riviera's practice range, both of us determined to work on our rhythm and fine-tune our swings.

Pro-trait #2: Jack Nicklaus

The Golden Bear eats the wildflowers of deliberation and concentration. And because he's a bear, we might say he digests some of the honey of healthy pride. He paws a powerful blow into both the ball and his helpless opponents, who are as vulnerable as salmon swimming up course. They say, "No, no, no, I don't want to be Bear lunch today," but Jack won't back away. His eighteen major victories fly off the chart of talent—not one of them won by luck. His swing plucks the wind out of hurricanes, and his famous flying right elbow salutes the unconventional signature of his greatness. But to see him in his essential bearness, you have to watch him putt, rooted to the ground like honey clinging to a tree. His bright blond hair shoots off the energy of a baby star, and his brilliance is mostly in his mind. Until the game finds someone as smart as Jack, why talk about breaking out of the bear trap of his records? This bear made a Tiger take the game of golf seriously.

The Meaning of Tiger Woods

You have to wonder whether Tiger Woods really exists. We know that somewhere out there a young man returns to eat at McDonalds as often as his taste buds permit. We know that a kid who played on the golf team at Stanford University for a couple of years enjoyed the kind of sitting around and talking with his schoolmates that, for many, *means* college in itself. This young man has always existed. He possesses earnestness, eagerness, and an ambivalent relationship to innocence: half of him wants to preserve it; the other half can't wait to skin its armor. What really preoccupies many a young man at his age, now thirty-one, is drinking a lot of beer and finding the "right" woman.

Our guy has the royal, even slightly anachronistic-sounding birth name of Eldrick. Eldrick Woods. You might imagine a career for him as the curator of an art museum. This imagined "Eldrick" possesses more than a modicum of athletic ability, although he has never competed in team sports since he prefers skiing, sailing, and, lately, windsurfing. Like most kids at one time or another, Eldrick found himself at the hurting end of his grade school playmates' cruel jokes. "Eldrick *Meldrick*. Eldrick *Hell*drick." This young man will have an ordinary life, with its private blends of happiness and sadness, successes and failures, loves and losses. When you get right down to it, we know Eldrick Woods very well. *Tiger* Woods is another story. And this makes us wonder if he really exists.

Of course, we have become quickly familiar with the *institution* called "Tiger Woods." Just as McDonalds sells burgers, the limited partnership of "Tiger Woods" sells golf. This business's business is to make golf as popular as hamburgers, and, with a twenty-one-year-old Master's champion as ceo, president, chief spokesperson (and primary *product*), it got off to a good start.

Tiger and his doppelgänger, his double, Eldrick, meet and mesh in one place and one place only, the golf course. There, Tiger sheds his corporate fur. There, Tiger becomes an artist, a poet, or a novelist chronicling a contemporary tale of education and identity that has its readers asking, "Just what does Tiger Woods *mean*?"

Tiger Woods Means Money

Why do people focus so intensely on the cash, oohing and ahhing at the mention of Woods's million-dollar contracts and seven-figure first-place purses? The reason is that, in America, people see money and success as synonymous.

In a very odd way, though, the fact that Tiger made so much so fast did nothing more than retain his amateur status. If you are not playing golf for a living, why bother even calling yourself a professional? The word *amateur* stems from the Latin verb *amore*, meaning "to love." Amateurs love their activity, just as Tiger loves golf. Let's hope that all of that corporate cash doesn't steal that love from him.

After all, we don't want our top athletes to simply put in a day's work for a day's pay, regardless of the amount of zeros attached to their labor. We want athletes not to "be like Mike," but to "be like *us*," and to play the game for the love of *playing* it. All great athletes play this way. It is hard to imagine such athletes developing their skills and talent to the level of a Michael Jordan without the foundation of their talent being their love for the game.

An assistant college professor in the United States earns, roughly, $40,000 a year. Such a person, with a PhD, would have to work *one thousand years* to equal the $40 million Nike Golf paid Tiger as an endorser *before* he hit even one ball as golf professional. Tiger Woods the human being might like to eat at McDonalds. Tiger Woods the corporation *is* McDonalds, and we eat it up because we need and want such a fairy tale—not because it makes our own lives more real but because it indulges our imaginations and sometimes even makes them more dignified.

Somewhere, in some pressroom, one golf writer overheard another say that Tiger resists taking a taxi when he has to get somewhere because he *doesn't feel comfortable* shelling out the money. Even Mark O'Meara, Tiger's former neighbor and still good buddy in Orlando, told a group of writers that Tiger often wandered over to his pal's house to borrow a basketball. "You've got some pretty nice endorsements," O'Meara said he told Tiger. "Dig down a little into those pockets and go out and *buy* a basketball."

Still, you've got to like this parsimoniousness in Tiger, because it shows that the young man has an instinct for self-preservation. It also offers a privileged insight into Tiger the person. In other words, if the people out there in golf fan land ever actually got to know Tiger Woods, they would see a bit of themselves in him.

Tiger Woods Means the Realization of Human Potential

"Character," the ancient Greek writer Herodotus said, "is fate." Eldrick "Tiger" Woods was born to play golf. His now departed father, Earl, had his son swinging a golf club before he could even walk. At age two Tiger was on *The Mike Douglas Show* hitting golf balls into a net. Earl has said that his son knew what a par, birdie, and bogey were before he could even count. "You made a bogey, Daddy," the pip-squeak would say, knowing his dad had hit the ball five times on a par four every bit as instinctively as a horse pounds his hoof five times at his trainer's command.

"But he couldn't count to five!" Earl beamed. In other words, Tiger was bilingual from birth: he spoke English and Golf.

The lucky among us sense a calling and intuit a destiny all their own. Some proceed and progress toward their prize more directly than others. A child displays an unusual ability to draw and can't put down the Crayolas. He or she becomes an artist. Thomas Edison once sat on a chicken egg for days, emulating a hen and trying to hatch it. A kid like that goes into the sciences. Eldrick Tiger Woods was born to play golf every bit as much as an acorn is programmed to blossom into an oak tree. Trace the records and read the interviews Tiger conducted when he was ten, thirteen, or sixteen years old. "I want to be the best golfer that ever lived, " he said in all of them. During his first win at the Master's in 1997, he may have played three-and-a half rounds of golf better than anyone ever had before.

Woods's meteoric start as a professional golfer ignited *our* imaginations, fed *our* fantasies, and kept *our* hopes alive for our own lives. We might not make $40 million at our job at the department store, but we can become a better salesperson. We may one day become like the forty-five-year old physician in Oakland, California, who finally told his wife, "Honey, I'm quitting my medical practice and am going to clown school. Then I'm joining the circus." Tiger took his first step toward his "Tigerness" the moment his father put a golf club in his hands. Our paths have always been there waiting for us to get back on them too.

Tiger Woods Means His Father's Son

We live in a world of absentee fathers—the executive away on a business trip, the factory worker holding two jobs, the entrepreneur on the phone in his office long into the night. Since the industrial revolution, both the workplace and the sidewalks of the unemployed have removed fathers from sons as never before. In that absence, young men leap into life from a platform of air.

Not so in Tiger Woods's case. His dad, Earl, was a retired military man and was physically there for Tiger every drive, iron, pitch, and putt of the way. In more magazine articles and television interviews than one can count, Earl Woods made what many thought of as outrageous claims. He called Tiger "the Chosen Child" and said that his son would "change the world." He added that his sole role in life was to raise Tiger to become not only a golfer but also a messenger of world peace. Some found such messianic grandiosity troubling, while it frightened and even saddened others. Yet how much easier it is for a child to become a productive member of society if that child's parent or parents from the start recognize his or her unique gifts and talents?

Earl also succeeded in distinguishing between his roles as father and mentor. When your kid breaks fifty for nine holes by the time he is *three* (at eighteen months, Tiger supposedly shot an eleven on one hole—*at eighteen months!*) and when, as a mere freshman in high school, he consistently beats the pants off of you on the golf course, you have little claim on the title of mentor. In fact, Tiger himself has told us that no single golfer served as his single source of inspiration. Rather, he took what was best in the greatest golfers of all time and integrated their strengths into his own dynamic swing and game. It may take a village to raise a child, but it takes a Nicklaus, Palmer, Player, Trevino, Floyd, Miller, Norman, Price, Crenshaw, Kite, Ballesteros, and Faldo (among others) to raise a golfer named Tiger.

Tiger Woods Means America's Demographics

The face of golf is changing, encompassing and embracing every sort of human being. Truly, the sport has become the "world's game." Tiger's father was African American/Caucasian/Chinese/Native American, and his mother is Thai, which makes Tiger so multiethnic that even the producers of an old Beneton ad featuring kids "of many colors" would drool with envy. From day one the members of Tiger's galleries look like they are ready to break into a chorus of "We Are the World." Maybe Tiger borrowed his white golf glove from the song's writer, Michael Jackson.

Yet people seem reluctant to admit that Woods's very first commercial for Nike Golf, where he says, "There are still country clubs that won't let me in because of the color of my skin," expresses a hardened truth that has yet to die hard.

"Tiger Woods can play golf wherever he wants to play," they say.

Tiger Woods can, yes. But can all people of color and women? No.

Via a Tiger-ignited discussion about race in golf and sport, the world has begun to change, and in this regard Tiger's father was right.

Tiger Woods Means the "Reclaimed" Eldrick Woods

We all have a public and a private face. When we go outside we put on our mask called a "persona" to meet the world, which is distinctly different from our deeper selves, those who make up and sing quirky little songs to a spouse or lose their patience quite irritably in a manner we would never show in front of a work associate or even a close friend, for whom we keep our very correct persona mask securely ensconced.

If we were to walk past the public Tiger Woods on a busy street in Manhattan or London, we would stop and stare at him. Were we to pass the private Eldrick Woods on the same street, we wouldn't even know him. Tiger Woods's true task is to preserve the soul of Eldrick Woods. Andy Warhol said all people would get their fifteen minutes of fame. Tiger has to hope for fifteen minutes of privacy. Our job is to remember that the Tiger Woods we watch and admire so much is, to a large extent, a product of our collective imagination and that we have embellished his athletic talent with a kingly aura bigger than life.

"All men live in suffering / I know as few can know / Whether they take the upper road / Or stay content on the low," wrote the Irish poet William Butler Yeats. We just refuse to see celebrities as real people—that's what makes them celebrities—even though we look to the tabloids to confirm that they suffer every bit as much as we do. In ancient China, when poets became too famous, they would change their names and move to different cities.

Yet what most impresses us about Tiger Woods may be just how clearly he understands and embraces his responsibility to embody a public image of athletic royalty. When he missed the cut at the 2006 U.S. Open at Winged Foot, he acknowledged, however modestly, that he was still in the throes of mourning his father's death, barely a month earlier, and therefore wasn't really ready to play. Almost a month to the day later, after Tiger claimed the British Open title, he released his grief by sobbing in the arms of his caddy and then his wife before dedicating the win to his father in his victory speech.

The reporters and TV commentators at both the U.S. and British Opens pounded Tiger with questions about his father. Did he miss the cut because of his father's passing? Did his father's spirit inspire him on to victory? While the daily sports pages and the sound bite stages of postround television interviews hardly seem like the appropriate places for such intimate bereavement, King Tiger's public mourning comforted (and one can't help but wonder whether Tiger intended it to comfort) us all. As he kept telling the media over and over again, "Losing a parent is something everybody has to go through."

Legend has it that years ago Tiger thought about legally changing his name from Eldrick to Tiger but that he decided against it. Had he done so, he may have reasoned, he would have had no place to hide and could have lost both Tiger's and Eldrick's soul in the process forever. Today Tiger seems to be discovering his own humanity in his very popularity. It makes one wonder whether this is how Earl Woods envisioned, if not orchestrated, it all along.

Pro-trait #3: Bobby Jones

The game, and the weighty expectations of his admirers, gave him a nervous breakdown, so he quit competing at age twenty-eight. He was a genius with a degree in English literature from Harvard and ones in engineering and law from Georgia Tech as well, but nothing rang Jones's soul's bell with more discord than this dumb game, where all the brains in the world fall short of the knowledge packaged inside the circle of the ball. Wherever you strike it, its curved side spins tantalizingly away from you. Better to follow the relaxed bounces of those other balls that hop over the syllables in a child's sing-along cartoon. Thus Jones built Augusta National as a place to play with his friends, where a wager for a beer was more fun than nursing the competitive juices of ulcers and putting twitches.

Pro-trait #4: John Daly

Long John Daly hits it a long, long way. But where will he find something to soothe his troubled mind? For his heart is as heavy as a wedge through sand, and his eyes are lidded from drinking. And his round belly forges a vault that hides and protects his childhood's pain. But John has charisma, and the goodness of the common man, the way Johnny Cash did, and I suspect they share many of the same fans.

Oh long John Daly, your swing's more graceful than Tiger's, and your power flows as freely as Jack's. Though three Gary Players could fit inside of your skin, his touch from the trap has nothing on yours. While he dressed all in black, your sunburned face blares so red your skin could burn the sun. You seem so sad, yet at the same time capable of having fun.

We pray for you, John Daly, Buddha of the overly Cartesian PGA Tour. Belly full of bogeys and compassion, though on the downswing it slides and pivots with a poetic traction not seen since that other working man's hero Lee Trevino held his proletariat claim on this game for one and all.

Pro-trait #5: Charles Howell III

He's so thin it looks like a golf club is swinging him. A polite young man, his tee shots nevertheless whistle like missiles.

Mike Austin, "Mr. 515"

Golfers everywhere share the fantasy of hitting the ball a long way. "What is the flight of the ball," Shivas Irons, the legendary guru and golf pro in Michael Murphy's novel of education *Golf in the Kingdom* asks, "but the flight of the alone to the alone?"

But let's shift back into reality.

It's the final round of the 2000 Mercedes Championship at Kapalua in Hawaii, and Tiger Woods and Ernie Els, two of today's longest hitters, have launched mammoth drives off of the elevated eighteenth. The hole drops precipitously down, and the trade winds blow firmly from behind the players' backs. Tiger's back looks as if it might snap with the degree of torque he places on it during impact. Woods's drive stops 378 yards away, and then Els slaps his right out there next to it. Big hits? Sure, and not bad for two strapping young guys hitting straight downwind and downhill. Now consider them next to Mike Hoke Austin's 515-yard poke in the 1974 U.S. National Senior Open Championship, which still stands in the *Guinness Book of World Records* for the longest drive ever in competition. Then contemplate the fact that Austin smashed his pelota nearly a third of a mile down the fairway at age sixty-four.

Austin, who died in 2005 at age ninety-five, lived in Woodland Hills, California, not far from my home in Alhambra, just outside of Pasadena. He once recalled for me his record-setting blast with his characteristic clarity, eloquence, and poetic wit (I recorded the conversation for posterity's sadly imminent sake).

"We were playing at the Winterwood Golf Course in Las Vegas, and I was grouped with Chandler Harper, Pete Flemming, and Joe Black, the best golfer ever out of Des Moines, Iowa," Austin began.

His own reputed prowess off the tee had demonstrated itself even before his *Guinness*-bound bomb that day, as he already had hit the greens in two on both the 527-yard par five second *and* the 532-yard par five fourth with drives and seven irons.

As the group crossed the street and changed direction heading for the fifth tee, Austin remembered Harper saying, "Man, I've never seen anybody hit the ball so far; now let me see how hard you can *really* hit it."

Austin, who even in his sixth decade filled out six feet three inches and more than two hundred pounds of pure muscle, estimated the tailwind that day at a mere twenty-miles an hour on that rather flat and fateful 450-yard par four.

"When I hit the ball," Austin mused, "it didn't go real high, just about twenty feet up in the air, and it didn't make a parabolic curve. It seemed to stay in line, and it carried 437 yards on the fly. Then it bounced on the green with the first bounce and rolled 65 yards beyond the green."

The tournament officials recorded the hit with a measuring wheel that calculated the total at 515 yards and 2 feet. "Forget the two feet," Austin said. "Nobody will remember that."

What was it like, hitting a golf ball that far? I wanted to know and was awaiting Mike's every word like a child being read to by his grandfather.

"It was like God hit it," Austin sternly answered, not joking at all.

"Who can hit a golf ball that far?" he continued, "Who *has* hit it that far? No one. I didn't feel like I did anything extra—I feel like I got some assistance from God."

The equipment he used—a Wilson Staff persimmon-headed driver with a forty-four-inch, extra-stiff steel shaft (that he said Sam Snead had given him) and a Titleist 100 compression ball—wasn't built to apply and absorb such supernatural force.

Austin pitched back to the green, then three-putted for a bogey five.

"I was disappointed" was all he added.

Mike was well-known throughout the golf community both for

his prodigious power and as a peppery raconteur. According to Austin, the very first (and only) golf lesson he ever had, at age six on his home island of Guernsey in the South English Channel, taught the secret of swing speed and unlocked a lifetime of legendary length.

"The pro at the course was named Callahan, and it was raining," Austin recalled. "When it stopped I came to the shop and said, 'Mr. Callahan, there's nobody here, can you give me a lesson today?'"

"And he said, 'Sure laddy. I want you to take this mashie nibblick and go out to that muddy bank, and swing the club into it. If you come back with any mud on your left sleeve, I'm going to kick you right in your rear end!'"

From that, Austin learned to release the clubhead swiftly and effortlessly with his hands so that it accelerated through the hitting area and cleared past his arms instantly after impact. The boy returned to the golf shop with his velvet coat, short corduroy pants, long white stockings, and Buster Brown patent leather shoes as spotless as when he had left.

Eventually, Mike's family moved to Atlanta, and as fate would have it, right next to East Lake Country Club, Bobby Jones's home course. One day in 1924, the fourteen-year-old Austin caught the great man's eye.

"Stewart Maiden was the pro at East Lake," Mike told me, "and he was teaching Bobby Jones on the left side of the tee and I was hitting balls on the right side. I was hitting them over a lake that was a 300-yard carry. I had a wooden-shafted club with kind of a suede grip on it.

"Bobby Jones stopped and walked over to me and said, 'Son, how do you do that?' I said, 'Sir, you're taking lessons from Mr. Maiden. He'll tell ya, I'm just an amateur.'"

Austin wouldn't stay an amateur for long, though cash at that time came in even bigger bundles after a "local game" or challenge match (with another pro or local club champion whose idea of his talent exceeded its reality) than it did from the official prize money on the PGA circuit.

All told, Austin won forty-eight long-drive contests and several tournaments. Throughout his long and storied life, he says he acted in Hollywood movies, sang baritone in the Los Angeles Light Opera, and took advanced studies in physics, engineering, physiology, and psychology.

But he was best known for the way he synthesized, integrated, and applied kinesiology to his execution and teaching of the golf swing. Kinesiology is the science of the body in motion, and Austin said he has a doctorate in the subject (CBS golf commentator and Champions Tour player Gary McCord knew Mike and says that no one is old enough to have been around to know if all Mike says about his life is true or not).

"Golf pros are dealing with a machine that they know nothing about!" Austin often exclaimed, with an almost holy quality of frustration.

"The body has six pairs of joints," he lectured to me rapidly. "The ankles, the knees, the hips, the shoulders, the elbows, and the wrists—and in the golf swing you have antagonistic muscles, protagonistic muscles, and synergistic actions, as in the pivot. A protagonistic movement is the initial acceleration of a motion, and a muscle can only contract, which is called protagonistic.

"When you relax the protagonistic, then the antagonistic takes over." In the language of conventional golf instruction, the muscles wind up on the backswing then release during the downswing. That's how Mike saw it. It is the release of built-up muscular tension during the backswing that golfers need to learn to accomplish on the downswing.

The only thing those who didn't believe it would have had to do was drive down to the Studio City driving range just over the hill from the Hollywood sign in Los Angeles. There they would have found a ninety-plus-year-old, white-haired teacher named Mike Austin, slightly limping because he had lost most of the use of his right side after a stroke in 1988 but still capable of placing a ball on a stubby rubber tee and, with a five iron, clip it cleanly and fly it right to the base of the 150-yard marker with his left hand and arm alone.

I watched him do it many times, and now whenever I see one of these iron-pumping PGA Tour players really unleash a long drive on TV—Davis Love III hit one 476 yards in 2004—I hold my breath and hope the announcer doesn't say the ball went more than 515 yards.

Pro-trait #6: Gary Player

The Black Knight's swing throws his physical well-being into the sacrificial task of smashing a drive down the fairway. He won each of his eight majors with the effort of David slaying Goliath and a brow stern with determination. This South African is a handsome man who fought apartheid when it wasn't fashionable to do so. His father went down into the gold mines and came up sick and died when Gary was just a child, and the pain that injustice inflicted has made him notice more keenly than most athletes the way the world's wrongs extend beyond the edges of one's own circumstances.

Now, at seventy-one, he still does five hundred sit-ups a day and drinks vegetable juice for breakfast, which may drive his wife, Vivian, crazy (though she loves to tell this leafy tale). But rest assured this health nut's gut is as hard as a walnut, and he's not trying to sell you anything but a better way to be. It's a simple song to hit the ball long and straight, which he hums by throwing his right foot like a base drum stick past his left hip with his famous walk-through move.

It looks awkward but surely gets the job done. How else could he have won all those tournaments in every part of the world? It's will power and grit that fuel the jets of this man's mind—as in the legend of when he was practicing his bunker shots at the club and wouldn't stop until he holed three in a row.

"Gary," his wife called out. "Come in! The President has arrived, and we're expecting you!" "Tell him to wait, " Player responded, digging his feet into the sand. "I've made two in a row and have one more to go."

Pro-trait #7: Fred Couples

Here's the man with the double-jointed swing, whose loop to the top and drop into the longed-for-slot has brought oohs and ahhs from crowds who line the ropes and grope after such fluidity. Freddy's shoulders, as wide as a bridge, span the air on either side of his ears, and he leverages that width like few before. Sure, Hogan had his hips whip his hands through the impact zone as if strapped to a rotating tea cup of an amusement park's ride, but Couples couples a vertical Ferris wheel lift of the club with a roller coaster drop of its shaft to make a whirlpool of air the way a speedboat wakes water to where the ball waits as in a white lace dress like a bride alive on a flowing green altar.

So when will the relaxed mechanics of this matinee idol's grace replace the thinking of the frozen snowman's brain the average golfer pains himself and herself with over the ball? Probably never, unless what's average, meaning static, dissolves into the universally sweet and spectacular motion of Fred Couple's golf swing.

Big Shots at Bighorn (July 31, 2002)

Golf might be the quintessential individual sport, so naturally fans preoccupy themselves with the question, who is the best player of all time? Until now, people have seemed comfortable granting the distinction to Jack Nicklaus, just as—until now—golf experts have rejected the possibility that someone eventually would challenge Nicklaus's record of eighteen professional majors. Then along came Tiger Woods, who, by age twenty-six, already owned eight majors, and by age thirty-one, twelve of them. Tiger quickly hauled his share of converts from Jack's camp into his, though some fans and writers, myself included, wanted to wait a while longer before we passed the baton, and its ballyhoo, from the Bear to the Tiger. After all, the title "The Greatest of All Time" designates lasting power, and while Tiger's fire presently burns brightest of all, the windows in Nicklaus's penthouse atop golf's pantheon still shine with six more majors.

Unlike most other sports, golf can pit competitors of vastly different ages against one another, as it did at the Lincoln Financial Group's Battle at Bighorn back in July 2002. ABC Sports broadcasted the made-for-TV event on Monday evening, July 29, at the Bighorn Golf Club's Canyon Course in Palm Desert, California, in a midsummer night's golf version of its old autumn Monday Night Football telecasts. The event teamed Tiger Woods and Jack Nicklaus against Lee Trevino and Sergio Garcia in a best ball contest, with the winners sharing $1.6 million, and I cherished the chance of watching in person the game's two best golfers of all time teamed together for the first and possibly last time. Seeing Trevino, whom Nicklaus has described as the "best ball striker I've ever seen, after Ben Hogan," and the talented young Spaniard, Garcia, felt like icing on the cake.

The match had a 3:30 PDT starting time in order to beat the desert heat, and the national television audience was set to join in at 5:00.

It felt more like a spectacle than a competition, and looking back, the word *invasion* comes to mind. A battalion of U.S. Marines from the nearby 29 Palms training base worked the event's security, and the troops swarmed the premises in the unmilitary-like garb of lime green golf shirts and crisp white baseball-style Nike Golf caps. Portable floodlights elevated on huge cranes stood in silent vigil over the last four holes, ready to illuminate the conclusion of the match should it extend into the darkness.

"These guys aren't golfers; they're rock stars," a fan said to his buddy. He was half right: they were both!

ABC Sports used its usual golf crew of announcers, including Curtis Strange and Mike Tirico, as well as Melissa Stark (who had an aide there to cover her with a shade whenever she was off camera) to conduct on-course interviews. Photographers and writers scrambled as if in a slapstick all-terrain marathon over an obstacle course of the sand, rocks, and cactus that lined both sides of the fairways. As five thousand paid spectators labored to keep pace with one foursome, I could sense the millions more sitting comfortably in air-conditioned living rooms and sports bars waiting to join in on TV. I'm amazed that I walked all eighteen holes with the foursome, but the risk of heatstroke seemed like a small price to pay to rub shoulders with greatness.

Tiger entered the practice area first to polite, almost shy applause, the way an auditorium packed with professors greets an expert approaching the podium to deliver a lecture. He walked between the ropes to a pyramid of warm-up balls, his catlike eyes focusing straight ahead. A faint smile and one miniscule turn of his head toward the ropes was his only acknowledgment of the crowd. He looked like he meant business, golf business, and though this was only an exhibition, Tiger's seriousness suggested his understanding that the golf ball didn't know or care about the event's status.

Sergio Garcia strode in next. Buoyed by youth, his feet so light and nimble on the ground, he seemed to sail over the emerald turf like a Hovercraft. Smiling and laughing, Sergio signed one autograph after another. Next came Trevino, talking and joking, his young son, Daniel, dutifully proud at his side, as if the impending golf game were an open-air version of "bring your kid to the office" day. Finally Nicklaus arrived, to the loudest cheers, with Steve, his strapping blond grown son, carrying Jack's bag.

Nicklaus has increased his popularity among golf fans over the years with his friendlier ways. As his monumental skills have waned, an unexpected self-depreciating sense of humor and humility have emerged in his public persona, which have only endeared him to the fans and media. Before warming up for the day's match, Jack did a TV interview with a hornet's nest of print journalists crowded around him. As soon as the camera's red light went off, a harried tournament official rushed in, like a referee separating two boxers, and said, "That's all, that's enough, the interview is over." Nicklaus just ignored him and patiently answered question after question from the disheveled writers (myself included) already wilting from the heat, with perspiration plastering hair across our middle-aged foreheads, tinted pale by too many hours crouched under an office cubicle's fluorescent lights. Nobody tells Jack Nicklaus what to do, even on a made-for-TV golf course like this one.

Behind Jack on the range, golf balls exploded off of Tiger Woods's clubface with a shrill whistling sound.

Finally, it was show time. "Hit and go," one of the directors said to the players, queuing them to hit their tee shots on the opening hole as the cameras panned in after a commercial.

"If it were 'Hit and go,'" said the quick-witted Trevino, finishing his sentence while striking the ball, "I'd'a been gone a lonnnggg time ago."

Watching Tiger and Jack play side-by-side felt like walking through the Metropolitan Museum of Art, where the individual painters express themselves and their times very differently.

At address, Nicklaus looked like a carved stone monument of his moniker, the Bear. Still strong and solid at sixty-two, he lorded over the ball with the immovable patience of a blond Buddha. Tiger appeared lighter on his feet, a sprinter more than a marathon man, and you could see where each man stored his power and energy: Nicklaus in his tree-trunk thighs and his hammer-strong glutes, Tiger in his broad shoulders and unbreakable back.

Jack's and Tiger's grips almost mirrored each other's. Both used the interlocking grip, with the little fingers of the right hand entwined with the forefingers of the left. Once thought suitable only for small hands (like Jack's), the interlocking grip continues to secure the club and the hands of countless other top pros, including Tom Kite, John Daly, Nancy Lopez, and Bruce Lietzke. Both Woods and Nicklaus position their hands very close together on the club for ultimate control and to prevent the hands from slipping under the tremendous force they generate at impact.

Nicklaus used his legs more in his swing than Tiger did, and to accommodate this lower bodywork, he allowed his left heel to lift off the ground during his backswing. While this gave Jack's swing a slightly anachronistic look, I couldn't help but marvel at the wonderful rhythm of Nicklaus's motion, which blended the agility of Fred Astaire and the force of Joe Louis. While Jack clearly paid homage to the classic swings of his predecessors Bobby Jones and Sam Snead, his upright swing plane coupled with his leg drive put the finishing touches on the so-called modern swing fathered a generation earlier by the great Byron Nelson.

Tiger shifted his weight in a more lateral rocking fashion during his backswing and then ripped into the ball with the hunger of a cat devouring its prey. His blinding slash, powered by his massive upper body, appeared to channel young Arnold Palmer's. However, whereas Arnold hit the ball low, Woods's shots towered explosively, like rockets that didn't want to return to earth. His drives seemed to swim in the wake of the ones Nicklaus hit thirty years ago.

"How would Tiger have done if he were playing in 1970?" a reporter asked Lee Trevino during the postround press conference.

"I think Jack would have handled him," Trevino answered with candor and measured ambiguity. "But I couldn't have," he added. "I had enough on my hands trying to keep up with this guy right here," he said, motioning to Nicklaus two chairs away.

Woods and Nicklaus played extremely well during the match, and both teams provided marvelous golf, with birdies winning each of the first fifteen holes. Nicklaus and Woods emerged victorious, closing the game out on the sixteenth hole.

"I told Tiger before the round to play hard, because I didn't know how long I could last, " Nicklaus confessed. Then Melissa Stark asked Tiger, "What's was the best thing for you about today's match?" expecting he'd take the bait and say it was playing with Jack.

"We won!" Woods beamed.

In a moment not meant for the camera or microphone, Nicklaus leaned over and whispered to Tiger that his half of the $1.6 million winnings represented "the biggest check I ever made in a golf match or tournament."

"Really?" a slightly embarrassed Woods responded, as if the $800,000 in question were Internet café change for kids of his generation.

At the end of the day, it was the 107-degree heat that got the last laugh.

"How did the heat affect you?" a writer asked Nicklaus, who was reviving himself in the air-conditioned press tent.

"It was the hottest day in which I ever played," he said. "When I drove up to the course, the sign said 117."

"Wait a minute, Jack," Trevino interrupted. "That wasn't the temperature; that was the *time!*"

Everyone laughed. I hustled out of the pressroom into the desert night and a long ride home to LA, hoping that my VCR had successfully captured this historic round on tape.

Pro-trait #8: Craig Stadler

Grump and splash, behold the mustached walrus playing golf. Only it doesn't seem like this rounded soul is playing a game at all. Clothes hanging from his hip with a slow hop that's fashionably hefty, here's an unlikely artist, like a left playing second base, with existential eyes rooted to the ground like a retired accountant combing the beach for rings and coins. "Stads," as his Tour cronies call him, demonstrates how the game tortures even the most feeling-full souls.

It's an unmercifully unkind version of democracy. Why? Because the bright course unfolds like a green cat stretching in the morning sun that paws at the ball to keep it from falling into the hole, inside of which hides the cannon of darkness's mythologies. Even so, those who know the Walrus off the course perceive his whiskers as warm and even friendly, and not the slashing/grinning blades of a warrior aroused by battle.

It isn't that nice guys finish last; it's that this beast's beauty won't flash until he's past the 18th flag. So don't trust sea-faring mammals that play human games, because competition turns their warm blood overly serious while a sandwich of sardines on rye bread washed down by a cold beer flutters their flippers and makes them almost delirious.

Pro-trait #9: Raymond Floyd's Swing

Like the earthiness of a bagel pressed against sea-born lox, golf embraces many a paradox. Consider Raymond Floyd's swing, which wiggles and flip-flops like a penguin climbing out of water. It's a motion whose intelligence is rooted in the feet that shuffle impatiently as if Ray's mind were trying to find words that rhyme with rhythm and timing. Yet, like Essa Pekka Salonen conducting the LA Philharmonic (no, I'm not trying to be sardonic), every genius sings uniquely.

So if Sam Snead paced his swing to the buttery contours of a comfortable waltz, Floyd waved his clubs in the more angular weavings of Stravinsky. But what matters most is that both men's swings approached the ball on the lyrical wings of a perfect arc, before they smashed it as if with the sweeping click of a massive clock.

Pro-trait #10: Annika Sorenstam

Where's the plug that sets this machine in such repeating motion? And how, with such perfect impact, can her swing break golf's first golden rule? Don't they say the head should stay steady as a rock? But she lets hers cock to the left just before hitting the ball, and looks to the left prior to impact, as if to see where the ball will surely go before it gets there. Is this the gesture of a woman set on disrupting the authority of golf instruction's male-dominated hegemony? Or is it, rather, a headless version of "look ma, no hands"?

Her Swedish blue eyes click forward like a metronome in a rhythm so timed and precise her opponents might as well chase her over ice, while the rest of us struggle for motion's freedom by rehashing tip after tip that, kinesthetically speaking, only slows us down. Annika's swing sings the anthem of finding your own way and points us toward a confidence that experience but no book can give—and that's as rebellious a formula as water rushing freely from a sieve.

Can You Have Too Much Love?

To the casual golfer looking for the next hot tip or training aid, the name "Ben Doyle" doesn't ring golf guru bells, as might other names. Nor is he related to Allen Doyle, though as a Canadian, Ben might like the Champions Tour player's compact, hockey-like swing. You might be surprised to know that Ben Doyle is one of the most sought after instructors in the game.

"I've never known anyone who understands the essential elements of the golf swing better," says Bobby Clampett, a former PGA Tour star and now CBS Sports golf commentator who, as a thirteen-year-old, began learning the game from Ben.

Ever since he began caddying at Vancouver Golf Club in British Columbia at age nine, Ben Doyle has been studying the golf swing. In 1969 he met Homer Kelley, a former Boeing engineer who had just completed a book that analyzed the golf swing through principles of geometry and physics. That book was *The Golfing Machine*.

Doyle became Kelley's first authorized instructor of the information packed into this seminal, comprehensive book and is acknowledged as one of its leading experts.

"He's the King of the Machinists," Andy Cude, a PGA of America member and director of the Quail Lodge Golf Club in Carmel Valley, California, where Doyle has taught for more than thirty years, told me. Indeed PGA Tour pros—such as Clampett, Steve Elkington, Bob Tway, Scott Verplank, Tom Kite, and Paul Azinger, to name a few—as well as countless amateurs from around the country and world (not to mention legions of golf instructors, domestic and international, looking to learn to teach the game better) have made the pilgrimage to Quail Lodge to work with Doyle. They may come waddling in with swings as restricted as those tuxedoed-looking creatures in *March of the Penguins*, but their swings leave Ben on the fluid wings of swans.

"Ben has forgotten more about the golf swing than most people will ever know," Cude points out, "but you don't have to be into *The Golfing Machine* to take a lesson with Ben."

A youthful-looking seventy-two, with a shock of gray hair, Doyle teaches with a gentle, poetic gleam in his eye that reveals his sensitive nature. He arrives each day at his "office," a roughly ten-square-yard patch of close-cropped turf at the far end of the driving range, in a golf cart laden with teaching aids and props. These include a hockey stick (for demonstrating the proper clubface rotation), plastic milk crates (on which students stand to learn footwork and balance), and a faithful video camera, tripod, and monitor.

"Isn't it nice to know that the swing has twenty-four fundamentals?" Doyle likes to say, referring to Kelley's segmentation of the swing into component parts, such as the grip, hip action, shoulder turn, swing-plane angles, and release motions.

"And isn't it nice to know there are only three imperatives?" he adds. According to *The Golfing Machine*, they are (1) a flat left wrist at impact (as opposed to a bent one, which would make clubhead control at impact erratic), (2) a clubhead lag pressure point (meaning that point against the right forefinger that feels the club's weight during the downswing and directs its power into the ball), and (3) a straight plane line (meaning a swing oriented in one direction through the impact zone, not one that starts out to the right or left and then *bends* the plane line back toward the target midswing).

I've spoken about Ben with Brian Leroy, an attorney from Calgary, Canada, who, along with his wife, Karen, has been making an annual trek south to take lessons with Ben for the past fifteen years.

"Ben cares more about you being a good golfer than you do; a lesson with Ben is a great event in your life!" Brian told me.

I can attest to that myself. During one of my own lessons with Ben, a cold, relentless Northern California rain was pelting both of us mercilessly.

"Let's get out of here," I said. "My sweater is so waterlogged, I feel like I'm swinging Vijay Singh's weighted training driver."

But Ben just kept referring to the rain as "drops of divinity" and urged me to "raise my sights," to a more optimistic place, I suppose, above the clouds where the sun always shines.

Ben leaves no method of teaching unexplored.

"One day, he had my wife and me under a tree swinging long-stemmed flowers, " Leroy recalls.

"If you swung the flower correctly with lag, its head would lag behind the stem in the downswing, then snap off at the bottom, but if you didn't, it would waver around unevenly and not break from its stem." Lesson learned.

Speaking of lag, which Homer Kelley calls "the secret of golf," someone once asked Ben if you can have too much of it.

"Can you have too much love?" Ben poignantly replied. "Can a boat be too buoyant?"

Are *The Golfing Machine* principles too difficult to learn, even from Ben Doyle? When you multiply and match the "machine's" twenty-four swing components with each component's possible variations (between three and fifteen for each one), then calculate the combinations exponentially, you wind up with one trillion, five hundred twelve billion and five hundred million possible ways to swing a golf club, give or take a few.

This has led some to conclude that *The Golfing Machine* is too complicated a book. Ben calmly counters that criticism by quoting Homer Kelley, who said, "Complexity is better than mystery, and a guided journey is better than a blind one."

Blinded by ignorance might be how Doyle would describe the majority of golfers playing the game today.

"Sure, people hit good shots once in a while, by accident," says my own golf teacher Gregg McHatton, who spent many an hour on the lesson tee with Ben, improving his own game and learning how to better teach golf to others. "And it's a good thing that they do, because if they had to rely on skill alone to hit the ball well, people would walk away from golf in droves."

I recall sitting with Ben in his golf cart at Quail Lodge, contemplating the swings of the golfers on his range.

"Look at all of these golfers," he said, "they're whacking at the ball, hacking at it!"

Even under Ben's tutelage, one doesn't easily translate golf knowledge into golf power.

"I remember after one lesson I became very excited and told Ben, 'I really understand what you've been teaching me!'" Brian Leroy remembers.

"No, you don't," Ben said to him sternly. "If you understood it, you could apply it!"

It's for the sake of application alone that Ben has his students master the chip and pitch shots first before allowing them to take full swings.

Gregg McHatton recalls the story of another one of Ben's students who, after an hour-long lesson of hitting short pitch shots with Ben, went to play a round at nearby Spyglass Hill.

The man came running back to Ben late in the afternoon and exclaimed, "Ben, I just shot a 78 at Spyglass; it was the best round of my life!"

Evidently, Ben told this student, "I would have preferred that you played the entire round by only hitting pitch shots. You would have shot 300, but you would have been *so good at it*."

I understand the man never came back to Ben for another lesson.

Pro-trait #11: Se Ri Pak

Who has the best swing in golf? It's Se Ri Pak. Why? Because of the smooth and silky way she takes it back. Sam Snead said the swing should resist friction like oil. Nor did he care if it belonged to a boy or a goil. Who has the best swing in golf? It's Se Ri Pak. Why? Because it looks like it grows from the root of a flower and that nothing fed it from a mechanical source.

"Who has the best swing in golf?"

A magazine editor asked me to choose one, and I thought, "Even a dunce by using his eyes can deduce it's 'Se Ri Pak's.'" And he printed it.

Canvassing the Course

Luke Donald expresses himself in precise and well-measured strokes, both on and off the golf course. Now playing the U.S. PGA Tour full-time, the twenty-nine-year-old Englishman, European team Ryder Cup member, and a top-ranked player in the Official World Golf Ranking is also an accomplished painter. He holds a bachelor's degree in art theory and practice from esteemed Northwestern University, where he also was the 1999 individual NCAA champion and Fred Haskins Award winner (given each year to the top collegiate golfer) as well as a three-time first-team All American. Donald, who turned professional in 2001, currently holds two PGA Tour titles, two international victories, and the WGC–World Cup title, which he won with Paul Casey.

I can't feign surprise at the confluence of these two interests inside the heart and mind of one individual, since I'm an art and golf writer. However, writing about golf and art is one thing, whereas executing them on Donald's remarkably high level is something else. While it's clear to me that Luke Donald possesses the kind of creative talent necessary to blossom into art-world stardom, after speaking with him about his art and his golf, I think that this soft-spoken young man is content to use art as counterbalance to the stresses and strains of life on the PGA Tour.

"While I liked doing art very much as a child and through high school and college, I also knew early on that golf was my passion and my direction," Donald told me. "Art provides a way for me to relax and do something other than play golf, and to live a balanced life."

Modest to a tee, Donald nevertheless continues to create oil paintings noteworthy for their confident compositional quality, masterly handling of oil paint, and bold, intuitive use of color. He has chosen golf as his main subject matter and acknowledges a comparison between his work and that of sports artist Leroy Neiman's.

"I enjoy his vibrant use of color," Donald says, "though his watercolors seem to stay within one color range, whereas working in oil, as I do, may allow for greater color juxtapositions within a painting."

Two years ago year Donald executed a golf painting for the 2005 Cialis Western played in Chicago, his adopted hometown.

"They auctioned it off for charity," he says, " and each day they put a reproduction of it on the pairing sheets for the tournament."

Luke took some time from his golf to offer comments on a few of his paintings, which I've woven in with my own response to them. Donald numbers each painting but doesn't name them, a common practice among contemporary artists.

Painting #1

"In college, I worked on an art project where I tried to capture the motion of different sports in paintings," Donald begins, referring to an oil painting of an infielder throwing a baseball. The painting presents Luke's talent and penchant for representational art, although he points out that "oil paint also allows the possibility of working abstractly." Luke orchestrates a wonderful sense of visual tension in this piece, not so much via the blurred throwing sequence but by the intersection of the vertically rendered ballplayer with the colorful rising horizontal bands of paint, which stacked upward represent the infield dirt, outfield grass, fence, fans, and sky, respectively. Also, the canvas's entire right border, an area corresponding to the blended colors of the anonymous sea of people in the crowd, vaporizes into a lyrical and abstract color field reminiscent of Monet's famous water lilies. This is the kind of textural flexibility inherent in oil paint of which Luke speaks.

Painting #2

While Donald mentions Matisse as one of the artists he greatly admires, the exploding wave in this windsurfing painting points directly to Turner, England's great painter of seascapes. The idea of motion has always fascinated modern artists. Consider the Italian Futurists' obsession with the brute force and speed of their burgeoning industrial society's machinery, or the American Abstract Expressionist legend Jackson Pollock, who literally threw and dripped paint from sticks onto his canvases while he danced around them like a possessed shaman. One also easily identifies an affinity between Donald's illuminated wave in this painting and the Impressionists, such as Renoir, Monet, Degas, and Sisley, who observed the direct play of light off of natural objects. This painting impresses because it reveals Donald's remarkably rapid grasp of the forms and flow of a sport with which he has had little previous exposure.

Painting #3

Though the two previous paintings lack nothing in technical proficiency and genuine expressiveness, Donald's intimate understanding of and connection to golf achieves a noticeably higher emotion in this piece, which, as Donald says, "is a painting of a friend of mine at the moment of impact." In fact, it's a whole lot more than that. Ben Hogan once said he pivoted so powerfully through the ball that he felt as if he were screwing himself into the ground. Donald's broad and bold brushwork (reminiscent of a group of French post-Impressionist painters known as the Fauves, meaning "wild beasts") in this painting cleverly mirrors the golfer's free-flowing release of energy into the ball. What's more, a vortex of rotational power radiates outward from the golfer's turning action to create a conelike cocoon of color that insulates him in a zone of perfect concentration.

I don't hesitate to call this painting a masterpiece, not so much because it expresses Donald's private passion for golf but for the way it hypnotically draws all viewers right into the very center of the game's dynamism and mystery. The strobelike spokes of the club's shaft radiating from and around the golfer's body bolster this painting with a little extra energy—as if it needed it!

Painting #4

"I was playing Cypress Point on the Monterey Peninsula in Northern California and happened to have my camera with me, when I found myself quite taken with the beauty of the 15th hole," Donald says, explaining the genesis (when he was in college) of this sensitive and beautiful golf landscape. He adds, "I also had back home a large, five-foot-wide canvas that I wanted to fill up with something, so I worked off of the photograph I took to make this painting." In it, Donald places the viewer in the exact position of a golfer standing on the legendary par three's tee box, taking dead aim at the pin across a rocky span of ocean. Yet the magic here lies in the way he also manages to divert his own attention away from the ensuing shot to embrace the entire setting of this Pacific paradise, with not one cloud, wave, grain of sand, cypress tree, or flap of a passing seagull's wings going unobserved. This is Van Gogh without the angst, or Cezanne with a six iron in his hand.

Painting #5

"This is a portrait of myself the moment after I made the putt to win the 1999 individual NCAA championship," Donald recalls. Images of a lion and a rose grace the bottom of the canvas, both emblems of his beloved England. "They come from the images on the pins I won in major amateur events like the Walker Cup," Donald explains.

Though to me this golfer's face in this painting doesn't look like Luke Donald's, it also signals how good artists often do not like to overburden themselves with representing reality *too* exactly. However, the celebratory stride the image of Luke is taking here, symbolically, out of the amateur ranks toward a promising professional career (with the benefit of a little hindsight) looks and feels spot on target.

Pro-trait #12: Tom Watson

Tom Watson's freckles, fading a bit with age, mark like divots' fierce spots the tick marks on the face of the clock of his career, which itself unwound with the precision of his friendly golf swing. Then came the putts, short, even shorter, just a foot and a half of eternity's terror. Such a pitiful error, as if each bounce along the green alarmed Tom's inner arm to reach for the ball to rake it back in. Oh well, no one stays young forever, and whereas hitting the ball like Ben Hogan while putting it like Hulk embraces two polls of a sad extremity, all golfers can relate to the game's absurdity.

As in life—the way a man may love his wife one moment with the tenderness of a star fading into the warm daybreak of a spring morning and then see shades of a dictator's mustache film around her lips the next. But each person had better supply his or her own images to illustrate golf's psychotic drama, as I'm surely in enough hot water with wives forever.

3

The Golf Swing as the
Axis of the World

Golf Mundi

When Jack Nicklaus was a boy, his golf teacher Jack Grout would grab his thick blond hair to keep his head steady while he swung. Maintaining a steady head and therefore a consistent spine angle throughout his swing has remained one of Nicklaus's most important fundamentals, and it has enabled him to play so well for so many years. It should surprise no one that the game's greatest player learned how to blend motion and stillness this way, for what else defines the golf swing but the magical resolution of steadiness and movement?

The very motion of the earth as it travels through the heavens offers a surprising analogue to the golf swing. Of all athletic actions, perhaps the golf swing best mirrors the earth's journey. The earth's axis—the *axis mundi*, or "pole of the world"—is an imaginary rod running straight through the North Pole to the South Pole, and it works as a suitable metaphor for a body at the address position. The rotund "torso" of the globe rotating around a steady, headlike axis stands for the pivoting motion the golfer makes during the swing, as if the golf swing and the earth's daily rotation were mirroring each other. Might this explain the ubiquitous passion people around the world share for this dizzying game? Golf may be the most popular participant sport on the planet. Golf mundi—the world's game.

But what resolves this dialogue between movement and stasis? Why can't the average Joe and Jane keep their heads as steady as Jack's? The answer, I think, is that people find paradoxes illogical and difficult to grasp. The entire golf industry of printed instruction and even golf lessons on the tee (with digital video cameras, weight shift scales that record people's body mass distribution as it changes through the swing, grip training aids that "beep" when the golfer squeezes it too hard, and so forth) seduce students into a high-tech dependency. The paradox of golf mundi simply posits that what keeps the head still during the swing is the swinging motion itself. "Motion keeps me still," the American poet Theodore Roethke wrote, and poets say things as simply as possible.

In a golf-oriented poetics, the coordination of the feet, knees, hips, shoulders, arms, and hands pivoting in a rotational manner keeps the head steady through the swing. If the body moves back and forth in straight lines during the swing, it is easy to see how the head must sway back and forth as well. The philosopher labels this duality of motion and stasis "time and eternity"; the religious seeker, "heaven and earth." And the poet, the one who loves and needs a little leisure time on his or her hands, just calls it "golf."

The Swing Sculpture

A few years ago I ran into a teaching pro friend of mine at the PGA merchandise show. I used the opportunity to share with him an insight I thought I had into the golf swing. I knew this person as a thoughtful man and a creative teacher. He had often expressed his feelings that people didn't thoroughly understand him when they thought of him as a teacher who focused on "the mechanical" aspect of the golf swing. He said he actually operated more from the intuitive, creative, image-making right side of the brain than from the logical and linear left.

So I figured here was the right guy on which to test my developing theory.

I told him that I didn't believe that the golf swing was a swing at all, because a true swing must take place on a single flat plane. Examples of authentic swings would include a merry-go-round and a tetherball attached to a rope swinging around a stationary vertical pole. Draw a circle on the top of a table, or take a round tabletop and tilt it on its side, and you have the basic golf swing's image of a round circle inscribed on a flat plane. But the golf swing, I argued, only stays on this type of a flat, two-dimensional plane from the point when it is hip high on the backswing to when it returns to the other hip's height on the follow-through.

Certainly some golfers have strived to swing on a single plane, not the least of them the late Canadian Moe Norman, whom many consider the best ball striker ever. Moe held his hands and arms as high as he possibly could at address, and then he tried to keep the shaft on that same plane throughout his swing. Yet even Moe's body, disregarding its portly shape, got in the way of his backswing, so to speak, requiring him to alter his plane, albeit marginally, once the swing passed his right hip going back and his left hip on its way to the finish. I reminded my teacher friend that he endorsed a swing whose backswing plane also shifted to a shallower downswing plane as the golfer made his or her transition from the top.

In short, I insisted, what we call a golf "swing" isn't a swing at all, because it cannot remain faithful to the two dimensions that define a swing. Rather, I concluded, the golf swing is really a *sculpture*, because it transpires in three dimensions, not in two.

My friend listened for a moment and then said, "You may be right, but you can't very well go up to someone and say, 'Hey, you've got a really great golf sculpture,' could you?"

"I've Got It!" (or the Madness of "Y")

I think I've identified the three most dreaded words in golf, and they're not "you are away." They're "I've got it!" Let me explain.

I practice a lot, and like a lot of golfers serious about the game, I have a "learning partner." My friend is one of the better local pros in Southern California, whom, for our purposes, I'll simply refer to as "Y." Now "Y" and I have a running argument as to whom the game has driven crazier. Sure, when I'm not working, I'm out there on the driving range where he teaches, beating balls for hours. He counts the empty plastic buckets in my stall, and the more he counts the more he feels sure I've gone completely nuts. But after all, Ben Hogan and Lee Trevino also practiced incessantly. Of course, I'm not comparing myself with Hogan and Trevino, except for the fact that all three of us have practiced for hours on end.

It's 1970, and I'm a freshman in college, which meant playing on the university golf team. Heck, I played all I wanted for free on the university course, and as a team member I received golf balls, shoes, and other perks. We went on trips, had food allowances—you name it. Looking back, I can see how college athletics taught me something about life. I learned that if you are good at something, you get rewarded for it, though my English professor at Rutgers saw things differently.

"Hey, Andy man," he said after summoning me to his office. "I drove past the athletic field this morning at 7:30 and saw you hitting and picking up golf balls. When I drove home at 7:30 at night, you were still out there hitting golf balls. What is it—some kind of Zen thing?"

I didn't know what a Zen thing was but was pleased enough not to be lectured for cutting his class to answer, "Yeah, man, that's what it is."

So my history of beating my brains out, quite literally, on the practice range goes back to my freshman year in college.

The madness of "Y" adopts a different guise. Every time I see him on the range, he greets me with the same phrase: "Andy, I've got it!"

Any golfer reading this, of course, knows what the "it" is. "It" is the answer! My buddy thinks he's found the answer to golf! And it's a different answer every time.

One day it is swinging the club back more to the inside. The next day, "Eureka!"—a more upright swing plane is the solution. "The answer is a tight shoulder turn," my friend declares on Monday, then on Wednesday, "The whole thing is thinking of the ball as a soap bubble: I just swing right through it!"

Now I'm no philosopher, and I still don't know what a "Zen thing" is, but I'm awake enough to see that every time "Y" discovers one answer, he immediately finds himself facing a host of new questions about hitting the ball.

I finally couldn't stand to see my pal suffer any longer, so I said, "'Y,' why do you think there is a single answer to the golf swing? Every time you think you found it, it ushers itself into nonexistence."

"Y" agreed.

The reason, as I saw in what might have been a moment of Zen clarity, was that there is no "it" to the golf swing. It's only a matter of time before you realize the "it" that you found today or tomorrow was the same "that" that fouled things up yesterday. The American poet George Oppen phrased what he saw as a particularly American obsession with simple solutions to complex problems as "the shipwreck of the singular." Reducing the complexities of experience to one explanation leaves a person emotionally empty—stranded, as it were, on the shipwrecked island of a one-and-only point of view.

I know my reasoning hit close to "Y's" own thoughts, because he immediately responded with, "You see, by swinging it back, rather than thinking about the position of the club during the backswing, I no longer lift it to the top like I used to."

I suggested to "Y" that the next time he finds "it," to catch himself. At his next epiphany, when the secret of golf presents itself to him on the wings of three or four consecutively struck perfect two irons, he might consider golf more as a puzzle with many parts than as a question with one answer.

What about my own continuing practice of pounding balls until I can no longer lift a five iron or think—let alone hit a golf ball straight? Well, I haven't found the answers to that question. Maybe it is a "Zen thing" after all.

Bashō's Haiku and the Three-ring Swing

A haiku is a classical Japanese poetic form that has seventeen total syllables in the Japanese language broken into three lines. However, attempts to write seventeen-syllable haikus in English often feel forced and awkward. The poets or translators of haiku into English have had to struggle too hard to fashion their poems in the "correct" number of beats. Writer Jack Kerouac had another idea. He suggested instead that "an American haiku" would simply consist of "3 short lines that say a lot."

Listen to how good the translation of this famous haiku from the Japanese master Bashō sounds in English, even though it has only eight syllables:

> *The old pond.*
> *The frog jumps in.*
> *Plop.*

The haiku hides a simple golf lesson certain to improve anyone's game. First, see how easily we experience this poem all at once. You can visually ingest it at a single glance, as if it were possible to read its three lines simultaneously. That's the first lesson: we must imagine our golf swing as one continuous and whole motion, not as a catalog of positions and technical parts. The swing is a circle, and a circle, by definition, flows uninterrupted. More on the metaphor of the golf swing as a circle soon, but now let's get back to the poem:

> *The old pond.*
> *The frog jumps in.*
> *Plop.*

We might think of the "old pond" as a golf course, where the drama of the game unfolds. By calling the pond "old," Bashō tells us

112

that it is a part of the natural landscape. He doesn't say "the artificially bulldozed pond." Indeed, how wonderful we feel when we encounter a truly natural (as opposed to a humanmade) water hazard on a golf course. Rae's Creek, near the twelfth green at Augusta National, is arguably the most natural spot on the course, as is the Pacific Ocean, which lines Pebble Beach's fabled eighteenth fairway. Every Ryder cup year, the golf media shrinks the Atlantic Ocean into a "pond" that the Americans or Europeans cross to compete on the home team's turf.

But Bashō didn't have golf on his mind when he penned his poem. He was obviously thinking about a frog that jumps in the water because it wants to. Even if a little boy were chasing it with a stone in his hand, the frog made a voluntary decision to jump into the pond. In the same way, golfers embark on the adventure of their rounds knowing that golf, like life, never progresses or unfolds according to anyone's plan.

Golfers everywhere have experienced the "first tee jitters." In fact, "terrifying fear" captures the feeling better, whether it's a 25-handicapper playing with his or her friends on a public course or a Tour pro waiting to hit a drive on number one at the U.S. Open. Much has been written about this kind of performance anxiety, but no one has said much about the courage it takes to leap into a golf round.

Bashō's frog takes care of that. It just jumps into life courageously. "Plop."

So, a variation of this poem might go:

> *The old course.*
> *The golfer tees off.*
> *Click!*

Here is an Eastern version of Hamlet's "to be or not to be" soliloquy. Should we break the stillness of eternity (the old pond) with our impulsive actions only to satisfy our temporary needs (the frog's desire to jump in)? Yet by the time he reaches "plop," Bashō's translator has masterfully manipulated us into an onomatopoeic moment, where the sound of the jump and the word *plop* become indistinguishable. The frog is no Western Cartesian subject contemplating action but a Zen messenger for whom subject, object, and action merge into one.

The image of the concentric circles spreading evenly and rhythmically away from the center of the animal's jump cements the parallel between this haiku and golf. It also provides a useful image of how to swing a golf club correctly.

One can think of the golf swing as the dynamic three rings of a circus, where the actions of the performers take place simultaneously. The body pivoting in a circle represents the first ring. Next, the turning of the arms and hands around the swinging body becomes the second circle. Finally, the clubhead itself, revolving with perfect precision around the outer edge of the third ring, completes the three-ring swing.

One has only to refer to the rounded shape of Tiger Woods's new golf swing, which he molded with the help of noted teacher Hank Haney. Another of the Tour's hottest teachers today, Jim Hardy, teaches a golf swing with a similar rounded look. Short-game guru Stan Utley believes that even a putting stroke should have an arced or rounded shape.

What's left but to revise our golf/frog haiku in the following way?

The frog plops in the pond.
In concentric rings the
golf swing's symmetry sings.

Fingerprint Swings

I was talking to my friend Cary, a fine mini-tour player out here in Southern California. The conversation turned to "the modern golf swing" versus the old-fashioned classic swing. Now my experience as an art critic makes the arrow on my suspicion meter quiver whenever I hear the word *modern* because the very idea of modernism in art and architecture ended well over a half century ago, probably with the death of Pablo Picasso.

The modern swings of which Cary spoke were no spring chickens either. They included those of Sam Snead, Ben Hogan, Gary Player, and Jack Nicklaus, who turned professional in 1959. Cary sees as the defining traits of those swings a lot of horizontal weight shift and a "reverse C" position finish with the back arched like a backward C. In contrast, he notes that the "contemporary swing" finds the body more centered and anchored by the right knee throughout the pivot, which allows for more upper-body rotation as opposed to the hard leg and hip drive of the old-timers' modern movement.

So I started thinking about the golf swings of these two eras and realized that the older swings had far more personality than the new ones. Why? Because the players who executed them for the most part taught themselves via their imagination, fueled by a trial-and-error methodology. What's more, I think that the older golfers were happier golfers as well, because, as Aristotle said, the key to happiness is to live a life in which we are always trying to figure things out.

Nor did these older swingers have computers to digitalize their swings and dissect every single muscle movement like a frog quivering under a high schooler's microscope. They had to rely on their own experience and sensations to solve the mysteries of the golf swing. No wonder their swings bore such unique fingerprints, whereas today's swing appears as mass produced as almost everything else in our world.

I wonder if some of the game's top stars can even go to sleep at night until they call or e-mail their teaching guru to get the latest diagnosis about their swing's illness (and a prescription in the form of a drill in order to fix it). For some, trying to figure it out themselves is the last thing on their minds.

I also think that the older golfers played the game in a more confident and relaxed way. Maybe depending on someone else to solve your swing problems creates helplessness, which leads straight to anxiety.

The bottom line is that the old swings—which I prefer to call "classical swings"—have a lot more poetry and personality, sculptural contours, yogalike club contortions, and nimble dance steps (that is, their swings look alive) than do the swings of most of today's top players. In other words, we've entered the age of the "technological swing."

Now I also see wonderfully unique swings today on the LPGA Tour, because like their classical swing counterparts, each swing has an inventive and imaginative look to it that is all its own. In what follows I've tried to crystallize the poetic essence of these classical and female swings and express them in a one- or two-sentence synopsis. Sorry to leave out the young guns' swings, but—though there are odd, weird ones still among them—for the most part, when you've seen one top PGA, European, and even Nationwide Tour player's golf swing, you've pretty much seen them all.

Classical Swings

- Gary Player's rollicking Buster Keaton walk-through follow-through
- Ben Hogan's flat backswing, which he perfected in inexpensive motel rooms with low stuccoed ceilings
- Gene Littler's swing, so inhumanly smooth they dubbed it "The Machine"
- Sam Snead's knee-squat position halfway into his downswing, as if he were milking a cow full of tournament victories

- Byron Nelson's club pausing patiently at the top of his backswing with as much virtue as the person it belonged to
- Arnold Palmer's whirlybird finish and peer, like someone late for an appointment searching frantically through the house for lost car keys
- Lee Trevino's stance and perpetual-motion address routine, like a hip-hop artist doing a break dance
- Johnny Miller's fastidious early wrist set, angular as the Tin Man in *The Wizard of Oz*
- Jack Nicklaus's liberating flying right elbow, determined as a fisherman taking off a rain-soaked sweater
- Lanny Wadkins's blink-and-you-missed it swing, rapid as a Hollywood agent talking
- Hale Irwin's morally upright swing plane, which considers bad shots character flaws
- Calvin Peete's empathy-inspiring bent left elbow, which turns with protean power into an envy-producing dead-straight ball flight
- Raymond Floyd's sharply inside takeaway, devious as a child on the playground at recess
- Gay Brewer's dizzying top-of-the-backswing loop, like a ballerina who has drunk four margaritas before a performance
- Doug Sanders's microscopic swing, so short no one could measure how good it was
- Larry Nelson's swing, with as many intersecting planes as architect Frank Gehry's Disney Music Center building in LA
- Jim Colbert's crouched setup to the ball, as if he were sitting down to have a conversation with it
- Bobby Clampett's swing, so flexible it makes Gumby look like he has arthritis
- Don January's whiplashing action, as if his driver were a sword in a pirate movie

Women's Swings

- Nancy Lopez's swing, with more dips, curves, shifts, and slides than a giant roller coaster

- Amy Alcott's swing, as straight on plane as the Golden State Freeway from Sacramento to LA
- Natalie Gulbus's huge downward knee-and-head dip, as if she's looking for a contact lens that fell out of her eye
- Annika Sorenstam's lifting of her head and eyes before impact, as if she were *putting in* contact lenses (as if she even has to look to see her shots fly straight to the pins)
- Paula Creamer's swing, with the club lagging behind her body so much that it looks as if she is walking to the green without it
- Michelle Wie's androgynous swing, built to pass on the PGA and LPGA Tours
- Morgan Pressel's swing, which pits joy and sorrow fighting with each other inside of her club's shafts
- Lorena Ochoa's swing, as carefree as a cloud passing by on a midsummer's day
- Meg Mallon's swing, which keeps such perfect time that metronomes ask it for lessons
- Julie Inkster's swing, which ascends on its vertical axis as nimbly as Jack climbing the beanpole to watch a playoff game with the Giant

Dream Lessons

"Ben Hogan was struggling with his game so badly, he gave himself three days to figure out his swing or he vowed to quit the Tour. The secret to his swing came to him in a dream."

—Gregg McHatton, 1991 Southern California Golf
   Association Teacher of the Year

A teaching pro friend of mine has posted the following sign on the wall outside of his office in the pro shop: "Golf Lessons: Series of ten one hour lessons: $700. Single lesson: $1,000. If you want a miracle, you will have to pay for it!"

That sign expresses the degree of frustration good golf teachers feel about students who take lesson after lesson, never practice the material covered in them, and then return for their next class disappointed that their swings haven't improved. It's as if we expect the information to seep from the teacher's mind through our bodies and into our swings via osmosis.

I've come up with a better pedagogical solution because, over the years, I have been receiving lessons in my dreams from some of the game's very best players. Occasionally, a non–Tour pro teacher will enter the space of my dream lesson tee. Quite often, nongolfers—and sometimes not even people but objects and images—will give me a lesson (such as the image of an airplane spiraling out of control toward the ground, which tells me my swing plane has become dangerously steep into the ball). But mostly the instruction has come from the superstars of the game.

Invariably, when I wake up and go to the range and try out the stuff they taught me in the dream, voilà, my swing and ball striking improve instantly.

They say that in life we all should strive to become our own best teachers. In my case it sure seems that my psyche has sifted knowledge of the golf swing I didn't even know I possessed and transformed it into the dream images of a virtual golf school staffed by Hall of Fame players devoted to helping me improve my game. Since these dream teachers exist somewhere in my brain, I'll claim them as manifestations of my inner golf wisdom. I'm glad they don't charge me for their lessons (it's funny how money doesn't seem to exist in dreams), because some of these same golf stars command six-figure fees to conduct instructional clinics at corporate outings!

Here, then, are some of my all-time best dream lessons and tips, and my efforts to understand their meaning, both in my struggle to become a better golfer and as metaphorical clues to help me live a happier, wiser life.

I received my first dream lesson about three or four years ago from Hale Irwin.

"What I want you to do, Andy," Hale said in the dream, "is begin your downswing by pointing your left shoulder directly at the ball." ok, that advice instantly steepened and corrected my excessively flat shoulder motion, which for years had whipped my golf club way too far inside my ball-to-target line, both on the way back and down and through the ball. Thanks, Hale.

The next lesson, some months later, came from none other than Sam Snead. The old Slammer, I was sure, was going to help me gain some extra distance off the tee, as I've never been a long hitter.

"Forget about distance," Snead reprimanded me confidently. "I want you to forget about the golf swing altogether and spend most of your time practicing your short game. That is how you will improve your scores."

"Thanks, Mr. Snead," I said.

"Call me Sam," he replied. "I look for my daddy when you say 'Mr. Snead.'"

Cute dream, I thought when I woke up, but I confess to feeling just a bit disappointed after the golfer many consider to have had the greatest swing of all time wouldn't share even one of his swing thoughts with me. It occurred to me that Mr. Snead—sorry, Sam (*my* father's name was Sam, so I look around for *my* daddy when I say that name)—was living up to his legendary parsimonious nature by withholding his full swing thoughts. But I quickly reminded myself that in my dream Sam Snead represented my own inner wisdom, so I grabbed my sand wedge and shag bag full of scuffed Titleists and headed to the practice green for some chipping work.

As I sit here writing this, I'm thinking about the comment Phil Mickelson made the week after he won his second Masters. Phil said that his game improved to the point where he could win majors consistently, and not just contend in them, after he stopped working so much on his full swing and focused on his short game. This helped me understand my Snead dream differently. I realized that the short-game and long-game swings share the same dynamics and fundamentals, so that working on the short shots, as Sam instructed me to do, would automatically improve my long shots. Sam's dream lesson was a pedagogical puzzle whose code I succeeded in cracking.

Some of my dream lessons have clarified certain equipment issues with which I've struggled from time to time. I wrote "Faithless to the Fourteen" (see part 4 of this book) because I have closets jammed with hundreds of golf clubs that I've tested and reviewed for different magazines. As a result I've become a hopeless polyclubist (unable to stick to one set for too long), and new clubs tempt me beyond resistance or restraint. In one clearly corrective dream, I found myself playing with a different company's clubs than the ones I had been using. Those clubs fit into a huge Tour bag with the clubmaker's name blaring in raised block letters off the bag.

Since I write about equipment often, and always strive to maintain my objectivity about today's gear, I won't expose the company's name that my dream executive stitched onto that dream bag, but I switched to a set of that company's clubs the very next day (it took me half of that day to climb through the mountain of clubs in my closet to find them!).

Another one of my dreams addressed the subject of club fitting, as if to tell me that playing anyone's brand of clubs means little if those clubs don't fit my swing. The dream placed me on a driving range hitting sand wedge shots off a mat with a club inappropriately upright for me, so that the clubface tilted so far to the left that it pointed at the wooden dividing wall separating the range's hitting stalls.

I'm well versed in thinking about dreams as symbolic compensations, as my sister is a Freudian analyst and my mother was a school psychologist (*oy vey!*). I vividly recall sitting at the dinner table as a junior high school student only to have my mom drill me with test questions from the IQ exams she administered to the elementary school kids: "What does, 'One swallow doesn't make a summer' mean?"

I think I replied something like, "Well, you have to eat more than one swallow's worth of food during an entire summer," hoping she'd get the hint that I just wanted to eat dinner (the smart answer has to do with how one can't deduce a general truth, such as "All bicycles have horns," from one particular example, such as "*That* bicycle has a horn").

Back to dreams (and lessons) as compensation. My dream's club-fitting session exaggerated the upright lie of the wedge to let me know that the lie on my wedge needed to be flatter.

Dreams blur the distinction between imagination and reality. Didn't the ancient Chinese philosopher Chuang-tzu wake up one morning not knowing if he was a man who dreamed he was a butterfly or a butterfly that dreamed he was a man? In other words, there is a link-like dance between our imaginations and reality. Our dream swings and waking golf swings only unite when we purposefully cross the imaginative bridge that connects them.

In fact, this cross-fertilization of imagination and reality doesn't limit itself to the "such stuff as dreams are made on," to quote Shakespeare. Dr. Jeffrey M. Schwartz, a research professor in psychiatry at UCLA, in his book *The Mind and The Brain*, writes: "The willful act of forming a mental image of a familiar face or place with your eyes closed selectively activates the very same face or place area of the brain that seeing the face or place with your eyes does." Imagining a physical action (such as a good golf swing) activates the same part of brain *in exactly the same way* as when a person actually performs that action. Popular psychology bombards us with slogans such as, "If you can imagine it, you can do it," although we tend to dismiss such aphorisms as oversimplified clichés. "He's just a dreamer," or "She needs to wake up and face reality," we say.

The only reality I face after a good dream lesson is one of playing better golf.

No less a left-brained thinker than Jack Nicklaus turns to the image-making talents of his right brain when his swing goes off kilter. In his instruction classic, *Golf My Way*, Nicklaus writes:

> Sometimes, of course, the "feels" and the shots won't come. When that happens, I resist the temptation to fire balls off like a machine gun in a desperate hit-or-miss attempt to find the "secret." What I usually do is pack up the sticks, go home, sit down, and think about why I couldn't do what I wanted to do. I think in terms of cause and effect. I reflect on my bad shots and determine their cause. By the next day I have what I hope is a logical picture in mind and a specific goal to achieve.

Nicklaus also understands the great French philosopher Gaston Bachelard's insight that "the imagination sharpens all of our senses." Beating balls indefinitely, Nicklaus implies, would *dull his sense of feel* for his golf swing. With all of the positive swing images Jack has pictured in his mind over the years, I wouldn't be surprised if he also dreams "lessons" while he sleeps.

Many golf teachers invest a lot of money in expensive computerized video equipment, although using video is just one example of how today's high-tech golf tools can shove imagination to the side. Sam Snead, perhaps golf's best swinger ever, reportedly didn't like to look at his swing on videotape for the very reason that video concretizes its subjects' swings into external rather than internal imagery.

Gary Player once told me during an interview that the biggest misconception amateurs have about Tour pros is that they have a completely grooved and repeating swing, when the truth is that pros are always changing little things in their swings as they try to improve. I don't think anyone had or has a more passionate golf swing than Gary Player, who looks like a conductor leading the Berlin Philharmonic through Beethoven's *Seventh* when he swings a golf club.

I suspect the reason Sam didn't like to see his fluid swing on videotape was that he feared technology would freeze its protean nature into a monotonous monument. It's no wonder Player speaks of Snead as one of his heroes!

"Responsibility begins in dreams," said the poet William Butler Yeats, because living (and playing) creatively requires that we honor dreams' messages, handed to us like gifts night after night.

I've had countless dream lessons.

Bob Tway appeared one night and, though taciturn in real life (or, I should say, on the golf course), he spoke to me in my dream loud and clear. I had been struggling with pulling my tee shots to the left, a problem Tway addressed directly.

He said, "You are flipping at the ball with your hands and wrists, which tosses the club outside the line through the impact zone."

He didn't have to tell me, because I already knew that this was what lay at the root of my pulled shots.

"Instead," Tway continued in the dream, "allow the turning of your hips to the left to square the clubface. The more you pull through with your hips, the less you'll pull the ball."

I'm not writing a blatant endorsement of the Andy Brumer Dream Golf Learning Center, but Tway's lesson worked perfectly. His talking cure cured my pulls. Sigmund Freud, father of the "talking cure," would be proud!

I wondered how long it would take before Arnold Palmer gave me a dream lesson. He's the King, after all, and I'm nothing if not a humble subject in my dreams. The King is the head of state, and the head stands for human intellect. So it made all the sense in the world that when Arnold finally arrived, his dream lesson centered around the head, around which the golf swing centers itself.

First, Arnold had me stand on two plastic milk crates and told me to make some swings. He seemed to know that I struggled with really getting the club to swing straight back and set more vertically so that the clubface didn't close excessively at the top of my backswing. Arnold expertly guided my hands back and showed me how they cock or set up without any tension in the wrists. I tried to do it on my own and felt the old grabbing with the last three fingers of my left hand, which shut the clubface again until it was almost facing the sky at the top. Arnold led me through the exercise again in the dream, moving my hands within his massive grasp, so that I could relax my wrists and allow the club to swing as if on its own on a more upright plane than it had ever done before.

But why have me swing on the milk crates? The reason became clear the moment I awoke. The milk crates kept me from swaying to the right in the backswing (because if I did, I'd fall off in a heart beat). In other words, Arnold's lesson taught me that a steady head keeps the body anchored and centered, which makes it much easier to swing the club straight back and set it into a more open position at the top. Thanks, Arnold—I can't wait to work on your dream lesson at the driving range tomorrow. But where am I going to get a couple of plastic milk crates?

Now the dream was also telling me that I needed to use my head better, to think more clearly about my golf game. It reminded me that the path to a clear mind runs through a well-centered body and that finding yourself through discovering an authentic golf swing roots you comfortably in your own skin. But what did the dream tell me about my hands?

That I must become more open and receptive to life. When my mind and body do find their balance, no doubt my clubface will swing into a more open position at the top of the swing.

To return to Gary Player, the Black Knight obviously recognized that I needed a little work on the use of the hands in my swing, so in a dream he gave me a great lesson in this department. That night I was walking around a beautiful golf course in Scotland with Gary, watching him play a match with some golfer I didn't recognize. Then, on one hole, with the sea gleaming just off to the right of the green, Gary stepped out of his match and took me to the side.

"Andy, watch how I hit this three iron," he said.

The Black Knight dropped a ball, faced the sea, and clocked one high and straight into the waves. Indeed, I saw that Gary strongly rotated his hands clockwise during his backswing (I remember thinking during the dream that Gary "clocked" one), and then he rhythmically rolled his hands in a counterclockwise direction through impact. The dream seemed custom-ordered to correct my tendency to do just the opposite—that is, work counterclockwise to clockwise with my hands, meaning shut to open, through the full arc of my swing. The second hand of a clock moves in the exact same direction as the hands of a right-handed golfer like me during the backswing. The image of the clock linked to the hands forged a marvelous metaphor for the role the hands play in establishing *timing* in the golf swing. I've been working on this lesson ever since Gary gave it to me.

After Arnold's and Gary's lessons, and as I progressed through my weekly lessons with a new (daytime) golf teacher, a curious thing began to happen in my dream lessons: the Tour pros disappeared. Perhaps they became angry with my seeking help in my waking hours, so they decided to strike. Maybe my inner contract for dream lessons with the PGA Tour simply expired. Whatever it was, they were gone.

In their place a decidedly *non-Tour* player, my friend Kevin, delivered the next dream lesson. "The whole thing," Kevin said to me in the dream, "is to think of the golf swing as a large, perfectly round salad bowl with an iron's clubface attached to it right on the rim. The clubface protrudes straight forward from the bowl's edge like a doorknob mounted on a door. As the bowl spins horizontally around like a merry-go-round, the ball simply gets in the way of the clubface's orbit" (that is, the clubface simply "catches" the ball and hits it very squarely).

This image of rotation, reminiscent of the old "swing in a barrel tip," ingeniously crystallized the proper in-to-square-to-in path of the golf club's circular swing for me. That the club on the salad bowl gathers or collects the ball *inside of its arc* represents the exact blend of geometry and physics golfers need to repeatedly hit solid shots. Crooked shots, of course, result from off-centered hits between club and ball, in which the swing arc and the circumference of the ball glance obliquely against each other like two meshing gears to produce sidespin on the ball in the form of hooks or slices.

But why did my mind conjure up Kevin as my dream teacher when I knew he hadn't studied the swing to understand it in this sophisticated way? I figured that the dream had more to do with the salad bowl.

In other words, I had begun to internalize a sound understanding of the golf swing that I had previously projected onto my Tour-star dream teachers. A subsequent dream lesson corroborated this insight. In it I was *giving myself* a dream lesson in which I told myself, "I'm finally becoming my own teacher."

The lesson placed me this time in a small rectangular room, something like a child's bedroom, and outside of the window I could see a large driving range. The room may have stood for one of those little teaching sheds or studios often used by golf schools these days, where the teacher and student review videos of the student's swings. But I mistrust militaristic golf "academies," where uniformed teachers wear khaki pants and saddle golf shoes and treat their students as if they were helpless children or, worse, dependent disciples drooling at their gurulike feet.

I opted to consider this dream space a child's bedroom. In it I began making practice swings that mimicked Lee Trevino's, and I can't think of a more independent-minded golfer in the history of the game than Lee.

"Show me a teacher who can beat me, and I'll take a lesson from him," Trevino once said.

As the dream progressed I could see myself lifting the entire shaft along with my hands and arms way outside of the "ideal" swing plane over my right shoulder before dropping the club back inside to the plane and delivering it back to the ball at impact. It was the old figure-eight swing for sure, and since I admired Trevino's swing more than anyone else's (with the possible exception of Ben Hogan's), in the dream I asked myself why I had resisted modeling my own swing after Lee's for so long. My swing yanks the club too sharply inside at first, and then it lifts to the outside and delivers it way too steeply, as opposed to Trevino's marvelously shallow wallop into the ball. Because my swing fills out the exact opposite mold as Lee's, modeling my swing on his would recalibrate my swing back into perfect balance.

The little room in my dream had a mirror, and in it I did my best Trevino backswing imitation, then looked up into the glass to observe my top-of-the-backswing position. Imagine my surprise when I saw that the club had fallen into an extremely flat or laid-off position (so that it lay in the glass on an almost horizontal or parallel plane to the ground) because in my waking swing's equivalent position the club points more vertically into the air.

Again my dream had shifted into its compensatory mode, and I needed no further invitation to work Lee's technique into my swing.

It turns out that my waking teacher, Gregg McHatton, loves Trevino's swing as much as I do. During my very next lesson, I said to Gregg, "Teach me to swing like Lee Trevino."

"You could do a lot worse," he answered.

On Phil's Watch

We all know that when the chicken crossed the street it made it to the other side, and that the man threw the clock out of the window in order to see time fly. But few golfers realize that when teachers or pros speak of the importance of timing, what they really mean is the challenge of feeling time during the swing. I used to think it hokey to see golfers such as Phil Mickelson wearing wrist watches while competing, because I couldn't imagine a competitor at that level giving a hoot about what time it was during a tournament round. But now I think I understand why he and others do it. It's to remind them at just what moment during the swing they have to focus on perfecting their rhythm and timing.

That interval is through the impact zone. Of course, that's a much narrower region of rhythmic conceptualization than most golf instruction asks readers to consider. Sure, instruction articles tell us all the time to swing rhythmically, which we just assume means that we must sustain rhythm and timing throughout the whole swing. But I think that where it really matters, or *when* it matters most, is through the impact zone, that kingdom that royally spreads out in front of golfers from hip height to hip height on either side of the ball.

I'm talking about the compound release motion that the left thumb, left hand, left arm, and the entire golf club perform as the golfer delivers the club to the ball. And this is where Phil's, or anyone's, wrist watch enters the picture.

The short description of the release motion works this way: As the hands lead the club into impact, the left wrist uncocks and the back of the left hand begins to roll or supinate to the left (visualize this by thinking of the palm of the hand turning up toward the sky so that it could hold a bowl of soup!). Because the left wrist has to remain firm and flat through the whole impact interval, the club actually rotates or turns through impact at the same rotational speed (RPM) as the left wrist. It's as if the left arm, wrist, and club were one unit like a pole and, just like a pole, the top part doesn't turn at a different rpm than the bottom.

So through impact, what we want to do is roll the wrist watch so that it faces the ball as we hit it and then let it go farther around until it points directly behind us just after the ball leaves the clubface. We don't do this consciously, as the supinating of the wrist happens as a result of the turning of the torso and the swinging of the arms, but what we do have to focus on is doing it *rhythmically*, that is, with proper timing.

If we lose the rhythm of this supination, the left wrist will break down and bend back at impact, and we'll have a cracked lever, or a broken pole, instead of a straight one. It's hard enough hitting the golf ball solidly with a correct straight lever (meaning the straight line between the left arm and the clubshaft), with a flat left wrist positioned like a swinging gate halfway between the two. Why even bother attempting to strike shots with a bent lever?

Lee Trevino has said that all he is trying to do is hit the ball with the back of his left hand. Eddie Merrins, Bel Air Country Club's "Little Pro," and a living teaching legend, compares the golf swing to a backhanded tennis stroke, with the tennis racket held in the left hand. According to Ben Hogan in his book *Five Lessons: The Modern Fundamentals of Golf*, what separates the pro from the high handicapper is that the pro supinates his left wrist to the left through impact and the high handicapper reverses the roll (and role) of the left hand and actually turns and cups it to the right through the ball.

All of this is true, of course, but it took Phil Michelson's wrist watch to remind me that the most important point on which to focus one's rhythm and timing in the swing is through the impact zone.

There's only one problem with my theory. Phil wears his watch on his left wrist, not his right. Since he swings left-handed, it is his right wrist that supinates through the impact zone, not his left. Oh well, this is a poetic theory, not a scientific one. Maybe Phil, without knowing or intending it, wears his watch on his left hand to remind right-handed golfers to roll their left wrist rhythmically through impact.

Of course, this sounds like an utterly preposterous preposition until one considers it from a quantum physics point of view. It's very, very unlikely that a person could run through a brick wall, but it nevertheless remains a remote possibility. If Phil is trying to help the majority of right-handed golfers out by wearing his watch on his left hand, I'll just say "Thanks for the tip, Phil," and practice supinating my left hand through impact, and leave it at that.

The Zen Puppet Swing

I had it all wrong all along. I thought if I understood how my hands worked, I'd understand the golf swing. Now I see that the hands don't work during the swing at all, though this is not to say that they don't play a vital role in it. What they *do* is nothing. Teachers have described this voluntary inactivity as "passive hands," the same term Jack Nicklaus has used often in his golf instructional writing. Indeed, Jack's hands did nothing better than anyone's. In other words, nothing is something, as the Arabs' great discovery of the zero first established. That mathematical breakthrough, though thousands of years old, remains a functional foundation of our civilization today, as the so-called Y2K millennium crisis as 2000 neared proved. Even months before the clock approached midnight on December 31, 1999, everyone panicked. How would computers worldwide deal with this triple dose of nothingness just the tick of a clock away? 2000! That sure seemed like a lot of nothing that everyone would have to integrate into reality.

So the fact that the hands simply hold on during the golf swing hardly makes them nonentities. Holding on is clearly doing something, because if it weren't, it would let itself be known immediately in the form of a golf club flung with all of centrifugal force's energy through the air.

The hands hold on and do remain passive through the swing, but they also direct the rest of the body to move, just as a traffic cop at an intersection directs the cars, trucks, and pedestrians safely along their way. Ben Doyle, the wonderful teacher at Quail Lodge, puts it this way. "The hands say, 'Come on shoulders, turn to the right. . . . Let's go feet, roll on your ankles. . . . OK, head, stay steady. . . . Now's your time, hips, turn aggressively through the ball."

In other words, the golf swing is a puppet controlled and moved by the hands though the hands themselves never move independently of the swing. It's a Zen puppet, like the nothingness that forms the underpinning of everything and ensures that the whole clockwork of the universe keeps moving as smoothly as possible. Remember the year 2000? It came and went without a hitch, just like a well-executed golf swing.

Telling Golf's Secret

I fell in love with *The Golfing Machine* the first time I read it. Written by the late Homer Kelley and first published in 1969, the book engaged my mind and imagination the way reading *Hamlet* did when I was a mop-haired college student back in the 1970s. Here was clearly the most fascinating and in-depth study ever conducted about the golf swing. Kelley, a folksy, self-taught engineer from Washington State, wrote the book over a twenty-six-year period, and he researched the golf swing from the perspectives of geometry, engineering, physics, and biomechanics. Many admire the book's mind-boggling, comprehensive treatment of golf technique, but others criticize or even ridicule it for being impenetrable, obtuse, overly complicated, and even unreadable. I wonder what that second group thinks about *Hamlet.* Even those who dislike the volume's difficulty admit that it has helped many golfers play better.

Homer Kelley hit golf balls regularly into a net in his home studio but played golf only once or twice a year. "I just wanted to make sure that everything I was writing was correct," he supposedly said.

While I can hardly imagine a reader not challenged by *The Golfing Machine,* I also find much of the information in it mystically simple. Right on page twelve Kelley divulges "the Secret of Golf," which he calls "Lag." This refers to the condition of the golf club as it constantly trails the golfer's hands and arms from the top of the backswing through impact.

Kelley defines impact as "the line of compression," by which he means the golfer's club, left arm, and wrist align themselves at impact. Golfers must compress the ball at impact. To do that well, Kelley prescribes the following set of alignments: a flat left wrist (for right-handed players); the shaft of the club pointing directly at the ball-to-target line; and the hands slightly ahead of the ball, so that the shaft will lean slightly forward of vertical. For comic relief, he adds that "hitting the ball is the easiest thing in golf to do, while hitting it well is the hardest."

Kelley uses the term "lag" and the phrase "sustaining the line of compression" interchangeably. In other words, to hit the ball solidly, you have to lag the club all the way through the impact zone. Years back I began to wonder, if Homer had told everyone the secret of golf, why didn't everyone who read *The Golfing Machine* instantly improve? Why aren't golfers getting any better? The answer, I realized, is that the people can't keep a secret. People can't keep the idea of lag in their minds—even though when golfers hear that "lag is the secret to golf," they assume that they shouldn't tell anyone!

It's all a big misunderstanding. Homer doesn't want you to keep the secret at all; he wants you to tell it to every golfer you know!

"Keeping" Kelley's secret really means never losing sight of the importance of lag in your swing. Golfers would be better off if they constantly repeated to themselves, "Lag, lag, lag." This would make the secret a mantra, or prayer, to the golfing gods for power and accuracy.

Lag is the only secret you can tell but also have to keep.

People have speculated a great deal about Ben Hogan's "secret," or *secrets*, since some say he had several. The secret most Hoganites have in mind, though, has to do with the great man's fanning or rotating his clubface into a more opened position at the top of his backswing. Most experts assume that he did this as a way of countering the hook, which plagued his early days on Tour the way the slice ruins 90 percent of 30-handicappers' games.

What everyone overlooks, because they couldn't see Hogan do it, was that this slight rotation of the clubface at the top of his backswing also dropped the club onto the middle joint of his right index finger, the very pressure point where Homer Kelley says the golfer must store and sustain lag during the downswing and through impact.

Therefore, Mr. Hogan's and Mr. Kelley's secrets were one and the same: lag. Please tell everyone, as I've done here—but keep working on sustaining lag in your own golf swing, because that is the secret.

Seeing the Light

In the song "Singin' in the Rain," and its eponymous film, Gene Kelly engraved the silver lining of hope into the psyches of many a chronic pessimist. But no one has done a similar thing for golfers, whose struggle to hit the ball solidly leaves them feeling lost and misguided. I've found that some of the best golf tips are short and pithy poems, memory keys that trigger a solid swinging motion. The great Gary Player likes to rhyme his instruction, because, as he says, "people remember rhymes easily." He says, "Swing slow for the dough. / Swing fast and you won't last." That's good swing advice, though as a poem it needs a little work. I think all golfers would benefit by making up one key rhyme or another that helps them swing their best.

Here is one of mine: "See the light with your right."

What am I talking about? I'm reinforcing the idea that the entire cylinder of the right forearm has to trace or point to the ball-to-target delivery line as the golfer swings the club through the impact zone. The way I've learned to do this is by holding a little flashlight in my right hand as I take my address position without a club, and then I simply point and shine that light directly on the ball. As I make my swing and move into the impact zone, I want the light beam to directly trace the length of the ball-to-target line.

If the light shines over the line out away from my body, the delivery path of my club would be classically over the top of that line and I would be swinging outside in across the ball. Conversely, if the light beam fell inside of the line, I would have swung the club under the top, or too far from the inside.

I needed to learn how to produce a golf swing in which my right forearm traced the ball-to-target line through the impact zone and,

136

more importantly, find a way to ingrain how this action felt subjectively. My way of doing this was by inventing the phrase, "See the light with the right," because though I may be a little weak in geometry, a glimmer of hope still glitters for me in the poetry department.

Bending Hogan

The Irish poet W. B. Yeats ended one of his best-known poems with the metaphysical question: "How can we tell the dancer from the dance?" If Yeats were a golfer, he might have pondered: "How can we tell Ben Hogan from his swing?" Indeed, to paraphrase Shakespeare, Hogan's swing has become the stuff that golfers' "dreams are made on." Considered the game's greatest ball striker and perhaps its fiercest competitor ever, Hogan seduced and teased the golf media and his fellow pros alike with the coy notion that he had found "the secret" to this most fickle of games.

With this in mind, two of today's most respected golf teachers, David Leadbetter and Jim McLean, explored the great man's mythical game. Leadbetter's book *The Fundamentals of Hogan* and McLean's video *Ben Hogan: The Golf Swing* analyze Ben Hogan's swing in close detail and interpret Hogan's own instructional writings (most notably his 1957 classic, *Five Lessons: The Modern Fundamentals of Golf*). Hogan buffs will cherish the many sharp black-and-white photos in Leadbetter's book and the slow-motion images of Hogan's swings on the video.

Hogan's swing was poetry in motion, and since no two people view a work of art the same way, it's understandable that Leadbetter and McLean sometimes disagree about aspects of Hogan's technique. The task for the studious golfer becomes synthesizing these two studies and walking away from them with a greater knowledge of the golf swing.

Leadbetter makes a concerted effort to translate Hogan's own ideas into instruction that is suitable for the average golfer. McLean's tape allows the film clips of Hogan's swing to speak largely for themselves, focusing the viewer's attention on exactly what Hogan said he did while executing his golf swing.

Leadbetter and McLean begin by examining Hogan's grip, and both teachers point out that Hogan favored a relatively "weak" grip, which for righties finds the left hand turned well to the left on the club's handle. Hogan's left-hand grip had the club running diagonally across the palm to the bottom joints (closest to the fingernail) of his left forefinger. Leadbetter points out that Hogan had extremely flexible wrists and didn't need to fashion a grip that would augment his wrist action. Most golfers, Leadbetter advises, would benefit by holding the club a little more in the fingers of the left hand than Hogan did in order to facilitate a greater wrist cock.

McLean seems content to leave Hogan's hands where they were on the club and goes on to endorse Hogan's advice in *Five Lessons* that golfers apply the major part of their grip pressure in the last three fingers of their left hands and the middle two fingers of their right hands. Hogan said gripping the club this way with the left hand "activates the inside muscles and tendons of the forearms," which, McLean adds, facilitates a free-flowing powerful arm swing.

Leadbetter also agrees that many higher handicappers would do well to hold the club more strongly than Hogan did (i.e., with their hands turned more to the right on the handle), because Hogan weakened his grip to fight a chronic hook (which he said "nauseated" him).

The great player carved a majestically athletic figure at address, with a straight back, barely flexed knees, and slightly extended though relaxed arms, and a countenance that seemed alive with the potential energy of a loaded cannon waiting to be fired. Leadbetter, however, believes that Hogan's stance was too wide for the average player. He writes: "In my teaching I've observed that players who are overly wide at address tend to overuse the body in a way that reduces clubhead speed and results in the clubface not striking the ball squarely."

McLean defends Hogan's wider stance because, like Hogan, he feels it facilitates body motion and, therefore, *increases* clubhead speed.

Rather than shake their heads in frustration over these contrasting views, golfers should experiment with the width of their stance and find their own best position. Leadbetter's book and McLean's video endorse and encourage this kind of trial-and-error approach to playing the game.

Hogan credits his "discovery" of the correct backswing plane as the key that unlocked his legendarily consistent ball striking. He imagined this plane as a pane of glass resting on his shoulders at address (with his head protruding through an imaginary hole) that angled downward directly to the ball. This image of the backswing plane, Hogan said, served as a "road map" for his swing, and swinging under this glass allowed him to place the club every time in the same position or "slot" at the top of his swing.

Oddly, both Leadbetter and McLean quickly pass over Hogan's emphasis of the shoulder-to-ball swing plane image, which may represent the player's greatest contribution to the literature of golf instruction. Both teachers adopt the contemporary view that considers the static clubshaft's plane angle at address as the guide for the swing's journey back and through the ball. They also agree that in a technically orthodox swing, the club traces this shaft plane angle until approximately hip height. It then rises above it until it reaches a steeper angle at the top of the swing, before it drops to occupy the same angle at impact as it did at address. Leadbetter observes that "Hogan's club approached the ball on an extremely inside path," while McLean sees Hogan's club swinging straight down the line as it approaches impact, which causes pause. Perhaps they're observing and describing Hogan's swing at two points in time. At impact, Hogan talked about bowing or raising his left wrist bone by "supinating" or rolling it in a counterclockwise direction. By doing so he achieved tremendous control over his clubface's impact position, which in turn enabled him to control the trajectory of his shots like few golfers have before or since. By leading with his raised left wrist into impact in this way, Hogan created and sustained the essential quality of "lag," where the clubhead continuously trails the clubshaft through the impact zone. McLean goes to considerable lengths to explain the importance of this flat left wrist impact position and the significance of "lag," while Leadbetter acknowledges its role in

Hogan's precision ball striking but speaks of it less enthusiastically than does McLean.

In a *Life Magazine* article published in 1955, Hogan said he was revealing the secret of his game. Neither teacher takes Hogan at his word. In that piece Hogan said the secret was that he fanned open the clubface during his backswing by turning and cupping (meaning: bending) his left wrist to the right. This motion, Hogan said, opened his clubface and allowed him to hit the ball as hard as he wanted with his right hand and side without having to worry about hooking his shots.

Both Leadbetter and McLean discuss this "secret" with some skepticism, noting that fanning the club open, while correcting Hogan's hook, couldn't or shouldn't be generalized into a panacea for a golf swing's almost infinite number of possible ills. This was *Hogan's* secret and not *the* secret to the game itself, according to Leadbetter and McLean. In fact, Leadbetter feels that fanning the clubface open can result in even more uncontrollable slices for many higher-handicap players.

Hogan sidestepped the whole mystique surrounding his "secret" with the cryptic explanation, "The secret is in the dirt: go and dig it out of the dirt." Sam Snead, Hogan's competitive rival, grew impatient with the hoopla surrounding Hogan's secret. With wit as saucy as Hogan's quips were dry, Snead snapped, "There are no secrets in golf: everybody's watching."

The Pathological Driving Range

Everyone tells you that the key to playing good golf is "practice." "Practice, practice, practice," they say, and "The more you put into the game, the more you get out of it." So I believed them. Even Ben Hogan said, "The secret is in the dirt: go and dig it out of the dirt." What he meant by that was practice. So I've been going to the practice range religiously since I was twelve years old. I hit so many balls off those damn plastic mats that I started to develop some serious medical problems.

I call them "mats," but that's being generous. A mat should welcome someone somewhere. These thin layers of foam rubber, with frosty films of some ungodful green plastic coating on top, welcome you only to the doctor's office. In fact, I suspect the American Medical Association and the manufacturers of these orthopedic death traps have been in cahoots for years. Here's why.

One morning when I was seventeen, I woke up and realized that I had lost the feeling in my left hand. That was the result of hitting so many balls off driving range mats. Of course, the numbness also may have come from the "Square to Square" method I had been so diligently practicing. You see, I taught myself to play golf mostly from a book called *Square to Square*, by Jim Flick. Golfers will recognize Flick as one of the best-known teachers around. He's on the Golf Channel all the time. He's been a partner in a golf school with Jack Nicklaus. But you'll note he doesn't teach the "Square to Square" method anymore. Little did I know when I serendipitously spotted and bought that book that it would become one of the most controversial instructional tomes ever written.

Flick said he wrote it because he had observed many high handicappers fanning the clubface open too fast, too soon, and too much to the inside during their backswings. That required them to compensate on the downswing by rolling the clubface closed through impact. This, Flick argued, required too much timing for consistent shot making. The antidote to the open-closed swing, which Flick considered old-fashioned, was the "new Square-to-Square" swing. He asked golfers to curl the clubface shut with the last three fingers of the left hand at the beginning for the back swing. Theoretically, this would keep the face square throughout the swing and minimized the need for timing. It also required a very upright swing, since one that moves up and down more than it swings up and around results in less clubface rotation throughout the entire swing.

What the Square-to-Square method resulted in for me was that the ligaments in my left wrist got so worn and torn by my pounding balls off those driving range mats that it took a surgeon to repair them. I still have a huge scar on my left wrist from an inch up my forearm down and almost to the middle of my palm.

Years later, after I became a golf writer, I had the opportunity to interview Jim Flick. "Look at what Square-to-Square did to me," I said proudly, impolitely shoving the scar on my wrist into his face. "Yeah," he sheepishly admitted. "People kind of overdid that method and got their hands a bit twisted up. I haven't taught Square-to-Square for years."

If hardened green toxic goo over a bed of cement isn't the ideal practice facility, let's discuss just what the perfect one would look like—such as the kind you find at PGA West in Palm Desert, California, just east of Palm Springs. Ben Hogan loved the quality of the turf so much in such desert courses that he spent his winters practicing at one each year. Those courses have perfect fairway-quality hitting areas and brand-new name-brand golf balls. They have target greens, putting greens, chipping greens, and well-groomed bunker practice areas. But PGA West is 125 miles east from where I live in LA. A round trip of 250 miles is a bit of a drive to hit a bucket of balls.

When I moved to LA, the first thing I needed to do was find a nearby driving range, one with grass hitting bays and good balls. Good luck. Sure, there were ranges that allowed you to hit off "grass."

But their grass looked more like a junkyard, where a canvas of mud and gravel sprouted a few anemic weeds.

This kind of a range is a great place to practice, if you want to hit from lies more suitable for mountain bike paths. The best you can do at such a facility is swat a few iron shots from the same spot, which levels the rubble into a smoother dirt divot that is a far better surface for hitting balls.

What about the quality of golf balls at such a "grass range"? What a tragic thing to find a bin full of new Top-Flite 3000 practice golf balls waiting to be scooped into plastic buckets in the musty shacks of such establishments. It adds insult to literal injury to practice with great balls off such terrible ground.

More likely, the balls at any driving range will look like prehistoric dinosaur eggs. How can you compress such objects? The objective of practice is to develop a repeating swing, and a repeating swing needs consistently good conditions in order for it to become grooved. The less compression these monstrosities called practice balls have, the harder you have to swing at them to hit them anywhere. And the harder you swing, the more off balance you become, so you might as well throw your dream of a repeating swing right through the sieve of your ball bucket and head on home.

What about new mats with brand-new balls? Is this a better practice blend than hitting dinosaur eggs off gravel? Let's revisit Ben Hogan's statement that the "secret is in the dirt."

A well-struck iron shot contacts the ball slightly before the bottom of the swing's arc. Then the clubhead moves a bit farther downward and forward through the ball. That's why when you hit a good iron shot off good grass, the divot starts at the front edge of the ball and moves forward four inches. You can hit four inches *behind* your ball on a mat and still hit what looks like a good shot. This prompted Lee Trevino to say that "everyone looks like Ben Hogan when they hit from driving range mats." At matted driving ranges it's no coincidence that the shots look a lot better than most of the swings.

Remember the scar on my wrist? As time passed I added tendonitis of the left elbow, a sore back and knees, and some mysterious generalized muscle twitching for which the doctors could find no explanation. Nor could they locate a source or prescribe a treatment to cure it, and they paid no attention to my question of whether it could come from hitting golf balls off of driving range mats.

Evidently they don't study the pathology of golf practice facilities in medical school. Occasionally I think about filing a class action suit against either the manufacturers of these mats or the operators of driving ranges, and I would if some of the golf pros who own or work at these torture chambers weren't good friends of mine.

Piano Lessons to Nobody

> "Experience, though no authority [book learning] were in this world, were good enough for me."
>
> —Opening lines of the Wife of Bath's prologue
>   in Geoffrey Chaucer, *The Canterbury Tales*

I've suspected for a long time that not only does the majority of printed golf instruction not help golfers improve their games but much of it actually *hurts* their journey toward improvement. Let me say up-front that writing this is problematic for me, since I have a lot of friends who are golf pros and they regularly publish golf instruction in top periodicals and books. In fact, I've written several of these types of articles with these pros, helping them with their grammar and syntax, just as they try to smooth out the readers' long and short games. I was also the editor of *Golf Tips* magazine for a few years, a publication devoted almost exclusively to written golf instruction. So perhaps I am a golf sinner at heart, and writing this is my way of asking for forgiveness. I've thought about putting pen to paper on this topic for years. Actually, the problem isn't with printed golf instruction per se, but with the perspective these usually nonprofessional writers/professional golf pros take toward it in their instructional articles.

First, what do I mean by "printed golf instruction is like giving piano lessons to nobody"? Here's the problem. Playing golf is an activity that belongs to the practical intelligence. We say we "practice" golf; we don't say, "I'm going to 'theorize' about correcting my slice." We say that "practice makes perfect" and then add that, "in theory, perfection is impossible." I feel a digression coming on, so I'll follow it. If it is impossible to reach perfection, "practice" can't logically "make perfect." Nor does "perfect practice make perfect," which is a marketing slogan golf teachers have become fond of repeating in their articles, books, and videos; *perfect practice* is as impossible to achieve as any other kind of perfection.

When we learn to do something that requires our "practical intelligence," we need a teacher beside us who can actually observe what we are doing and make the needed suggestions and adjustments designed to correct our faulty technique. This is what a piano teacher does during a lesson, right? He or she hears "C flat" and says, "No, it's C." When a student struggles at a certain point with the rhythm of a piece, the teacher models the correct rhythm for them by playing that section correctly.

If, for example, I'm not getting behind the ball because I'm not shifting my weight sufficiently during my backswing pivot, I need a good teacher who can see and spot that and tell me so right then and there. He or she has to say, "You're spinning your hips and not shifting your weight back at all, and so instead of moving correctly back into the brace of your right foot and leg, you are actually reverse pivoting and moving forward."

Countless readers of magazine articles have encountered this "reverse pivot" idea. But how do they know that this is *their* swing problem until *their* teacher identifies it for them in *their* swing? A two-dimensional glossy and perfectly air-blown golf pro on the magazine's page can't squiggle up from it as in an old Disney cartoon, puff him or herself out into three-dimensional space, and say, "Andy Brumer, *you* have a weight shift problem, so *you* have to turn to page 133 in this magazine because the editors have printed this instruction article for *you* and *you alone!*" Tiger Woods may have a huge endorsement deal with Disney, but neither Mickey Mouse nor Tiger can successfully give a golf lesson to nobody, and that's implicitly what published golf instruction articles often do.

Art moves from specifics to wholeness, whereas science starts with a general hypothesis—the earth exerts a gravitational pull on objects inside its atmosphere—then proceeds to *deduce* the theory's truthfulness by finding examples that prove the rule—apples fall to the earth from the limbs of apple trees, or people weigh more at the equator than at the North Pole, or whatever it may be, as long as the example supports the idea of the existence of gravity.

Almost all printed golf instruction today works deductively this way. This is why so many teachers, and the golf instruction industry in general, seem hopelessly in love with the notion that the game of golf is science. However, experimentation in the case of a printed golf lesson would have to prove that that lesson were "true" with *every single student who tried the lesson* before the scientific community would ever call that lesson a fact.

While golf teachers and instruction editors are certainly smart enough to know this just ain't gonna happen, whenever they get together at teaching summits with names like "A Scientific Approach to the Golf Swing," all they seem to do is disagree about how the club should be swung! Until every golf pro agrees on one way to swing a golf club and one way alone, it just seems like downright foolish ignorance, if not arrogance, to call the golf swing a science.

That these teachers' hero—nay, their king or god—Ben Hogan himself wrote perhaps the most influential instruction book of all time from the *completely opposite* philosophical point of view seems to gloss the discussion with an air of absurdity and, thank God, some needed comic relief.

The first step is to pull out Ben Hogan's classic instruction book, *Five Lessons: The Modern Fundamentals of Golf*, first published in 1957. We all know Hogan as an absolute genius on the golf course, but who would have thought (although why would anyone doubt it?) that his pen was as mighty as his club?

"Modern" and "Five" stand as the two key or operative words in Hogan's title. A central tenet of modernism is that (as the wonderful modernist poet Wallace Stevens phrased it) "in the sum of the parts there are only the parts." To arrive at a vision of the whole while maintaining the individuality of the parts that compose it also represents the essence of inductive reasoning, and inductive reasoning comes from the same instinct to observe phenomenon closely, as does the making of art and poetry.

Science breathes the ether of abstraction and theory, while art dwells in the materiality of the practical imagination. Most printed golf instruction is like giving piano lessons to no student because it is simply too theoretical.

This could all change if—rather than printing scientific, style-based golf instruction, which emphasizes the look of a swing by first hypothesizing its outline in a series of drawn dots and then filling them in via a list of authoritarian instructions—teachers would follow Mr. Hogan's lead. This would involve their willingness to observe intensely and with curiosity each part of the golf swing and then encourage and assist their students in composing them into motions in which all of these parts interact together. Such a truly *dynamic* golf swing, while appearing unmistakably whole, would nevertheless both retain and reveal the individual parts that compose it. Look at films of Hogan's, Sam Snead's, or Byron Nelson's swings, and you'll see a choreography of kinesthetic chaos that also magically appears all of a single piece (the old and sadly forgotten ideal of the "one-piece swing"). That's golf's contribution to modernism in a nutshell, and that was also Mr. Hogan's genius. And that's the kind of dynamically based printed golf instruction that I would want to read and would feel comfortable—indeed, excited—about writing.

4

Golf as a Tool Chest

Faithless to the Fourteen

It just so happens to be Arnold Palmer's birthday tomorrow, and the occasion has started me thinking about golf clubs again, both the King's golf clubs and my own. It's odd to consider that Arnold Palmer and I have something in common. He's known for his humongous collection of golf clubs, thousands of them, all cataloged and stored for posterity, and I have thirty or forty sets myself, most of them in a rented storage locker in South Pasadena. Some of them, my "A" group of sets, I keep in my study's closet at home. "Keep" may be too generous a word. All are tossed or strewn or hoisted onto shelves, or piled on top of one another haphazardly. Some look like newborn animals, their heads exposed and peeping out of shells of torn and frail long cardboard boxes, while others pose pathetically for no cameras in pastel-colored golf bags. The whole situation serves as a terrible indictment of my inner chaos.

Why do I have so many clubs? Because I have been writing about golf equipment for last fifteen years, and companies keep sending me their products to test, evaluate, familiarize myself with, and write about. It's all very legit. How many people write seriously about golf equipment? A couple dozen, maybe, in the entire world? I'm sure their closets, garages, and storage spaces sprout as plentiful a crop as mine.

Here's the procedure, which sometimes spills over into a grind. I contact a manufacturer and say, "Can you send me a set of these irons, or that driver, or your new putter?" Sometimes I hear a pause through the receiver, sincere in its brief duration, as if the person on the other end were quickly assessing my claim of being a golf writer (weighing that against his or her suspicion that I'm a thief). But, as I said, I can't write knowledgeably about clubs unless I try them out.

It's really no big deal. Should a movie critic pay to get into a movie theater? Does the fact that he or she gets in for free truly influence the reviews? Absolutely not. In fact, paying for the movie, or for the clubs, would make the film critic, and me, *less* objective: we'd want to get our money's worth and focus on enjoying the product itself.

The real problem is that having so many sets of golf clubs now—not to mention dozens of individual drivers, wedges, putters, utility clubs, and fairway woods—has made it very confusing for me to choose a set with which to play. Now I'm not confessing or conceding to any kind of professional corruption here. I haven't used my position as a golf writer to accumulate a small fortune in golf equipment. That would be a bad, bad thing. I wanted each and every set and club I have because I was curious about them—their clubhead designs and materials, their shaft flexes and blends of vertical strength and diagonal torsion, and their lie and loft angles; bounce grinds on wedge soles; and putters with different formulas of polymer inserts, not to mention putters with no inserts, mallet putters, blade putters, heel/toe weighted putters, putters with graphite shafts, a wooden-headed putter with a steel shaft, and a steel-headed one with a wooden shaft. Not only that, but somehow I seem to have more than one model of the same putter—including three Wilson 8802s, two Odyssey mallets, a few old Ray Cooks. I don't know how this happened, unless I forgot that I asked for one from a company in the first place.

Let me toot my exonerating horn one more time, although proclamations of innocence smell of guilt. Sometimes I donate these clubs to junior golfers who are not fortunate enough to have good clubs of their own. I confess that I haven't done this as much as I would like to, and I always say that it's because the shafts on my clubs are generally too long and too stiff for juniors. The bottom line is that these damned things are lying around like corpses as we speak, asking themselves what I intend to do with them.

I remember talking to my friend Todd, a local golf pro, one day on the driving range. He was just sort of standing around twirling his driver between his fingers absentmindedly, the way Fred Couples sometimes does, when I asked him what he was doing. He said he was thinking about which drainage ditch here in LA to throw his clubs into, and he was serious. That's just the way I feel and think when I come close to really quitting the game. My collection of golf "implements," as noted golf instructor Jim Flick so eruditely calls them, would cause a small tsunami even if I threw them into the Pacific Ocean. So here (and there), the sweet darlings sit, asleep now like vampires as the hour approaches midnight, the day before Arnold Palmer's birthday.

The Half-degree Solution

Years ago I was at a media outing put on by an equipment manufacturer, Founders Club, in order to publicize their new clubs. Though the manufacturer is defunct now, many an avid golfer will remember it. Of course, the story of that company needs to be told one day, and I can't resist offering the short version of it here.

Founders Club was Gary Adams's second company, the first being TaylorMade. Gary's pancreatic cancer, which led to his death at the untimely age of fifty-six in 2000, also killed Founders Club as an OEM (original equipment maker), even though the company had in a very short time begun to rival such established club manufacturers as Callaway, TaylorMade, and PING. Gary Adams was always way ahead of his time as far as designing and producing the best-quality golf clubs, and this company was to focus on designing products for better players. For too short a time, then, you had the best making the best for the best. It's no wonder that Founders Club clubs still turn up today in the bags of some of the game's top players.

But our topic now is club fitting.

The Founders Club outing took place at the La Costa Resort and Spa in Carlsbad, California. I was standing on the practice tee there with Bob Vokey, now known as the designer of Titleist's popular wedge line. Back then Vokey was the chief designer for all of Founders Club's clubs, having worked with Gary Adams during TaylorMade's formative glory days.

I was hitting my Founders Club–forged seven iron on the range and, wouldn't you know it, every single shot drew ten yards left of my target. Every one! My six iron went straight, my five iron went straight, no one could point as straight as I hit my nine iron— everything but the seven iron went straight as a laser beam. (A few years later I interviewed Sam Snead about his golf equipment, and he told me that he had a balky seven iron that he could never hit consistently straight—though, sadly, that's about all my golf career and Sam Snead's have in common.) Vokey watched me hit balls with his arms folded and then pointed over to the Founders Club equipment van parked on the other side of the range, which the company brought to the outing to impress us writers. Gary Adams was a man of class, and neither before nor since have I seen a club maker drive an equipment van to its media outing.

I believe I was the only writer to have walked into the equipment van that day. As in a dream, it seems that the equipment van sat there at the edge of the range just for me. Vokey simply said, "Go in there and have them flatten that seven iron one half a degree."

I said, "Only half a degree?"

He said, "Half a degree."

I said, "Is half a degree going to make any difference?"

He said, "Start with half a degree."

So I went in and told the technician, "Bob Vokey says we should flatten this seven iron half a degree." The guy didn't budge or flinch, and his nongesture said the prescription made all the sense in the world to him.

He took that baby, popped it into the vice, secured his bending bar around the seven iron's hosel, and tugged a little on it with the resignation of a senior citizen pulling on the arm of a slot machine in Las Vegas, before handing the club back to me. "Half a degree," he said.

I went back to the range and hit every single shot as straight as an arrow with that club as if it were brand-new.

Now I could have gone to twenty-five teachers and spent $15,000 on lessons to correct my hook. I could have attended golf schools in every corner of the world. I could have put my swing on videotape from thirty-seven different angles, had it digitalized into a stick man, seen it played back to me for an hour in slow motion, had it emailed to my laptop from some teaching guru in Orlando, Florida, had it superimposed for comparison's sake over Nick Faldo, Nick Price, Jack Nicklaus, Jack Nicholson, St. Nicholas, and every other Nick who ever made a golf swing—and every one of those golf teachers would have found a mechanical swing flaw in my action to explain my hook with that seven iron.

But I didn't do that.

All I did was *flatten the club half a degree,* and the ball flew straighter than you could point.

They said Ben Hogan was so accurate that when he played thirty-six holes of golf in a day, he'd drive his opening drive of his second round into the divot of the first iron shot of the first round (to which his archrival Sam Snead shrewdly asked, "If he was so accurate, why didn't he *miss* the divot?"). People also said that Hogan hit his iron shots so straight that the ball's flight completely covered the flagstick, so that someone standing behind had to step to the side to see the pin. Someone watching me hit with that "new" seven iron wouldn't have to look for the pin at all: they would only have to listen for the clank of the ball against it.

So what's the lesson a golfer can learn here?

That to find the holy grail of grooved consistency, we have to change more than our golf swings. That's why there are equipment vans at every Tour stop—so that the players can go in there and make small adjustments to their clubs.

Incidentally, during my interview with Sam Snead, I asked, "Mr. Snead, did you ever try adjusting the lie angle on your troubled seven iron?"

"I tried everything," he snapped back, which ended our discussion about golf equipment right then and there.

Strokes of Genius

F. Scott Fitzgerald said a genius was someone who could think two contradictory thoughts at the same time and still function, while Sam Snead liked to assert that a person had to be a little dumb to be a great golfer. An unsuspected axis that joins these axioms is Odyssey Golf's White Hot 2-Ball Blade putter. Soon after hitting the market in 2002, it became a best-selling club, with close to half a million rung up at pro shops in that year alone. It's perhaps also the most talked about golf club since Callaway birthed the original Big Bertha driver back in 1991.

One can't argue with its success among the pro ranks. Paul Lawrie brought it to the golfing world's attention by draining a monster putt with it on the 18th at St. Andrews to win the Dunhill Links Championship (he'd go on to win the 1999 British Open); Fred Funk has extended his career with it; Annika Sorenstam now dominates the LPGA Tour with it; Julie Inkster won the women's U.S. Open with it; Bernard Langer putts with a long-handled version of it; and Irishman Padraig Harrington outdueled Tiger Woods to win Tiger's own tournament, the Target World Challenge, with it.

Now to make a putt you need to coordinate, that is to say, think about two things at once: line and speed. At first glance those things do not seem contradictory, except that proper alignment is an act of geometrical abstraction; it's an image held in the mind before putting, whereas putting the ball at the correct speed is an act of physics. Snead, who may have been a genius, and who knew it did you no good to think too much while you were playing golf, would have loved the 2-Ball putter. Its two white concentric alignment discs on top of the club align golfers so well to the intended line that the putter frees golfers to think only about speed. Two heads may be better than one, but "the right" thought is definitely helped by the two ball on this singular clubhead.

Actually, there once were three balls on a putter. Short-game guru Dave Pelz's 3-Ball putter was popular on the Tour in the mid-1980s. Nebraskan Tom Sieckmann had great success with the putter on the Tour, which may have contributed to the wistfulness in Pelz's voice when he mentions that nine players had 3-Ball putters in their bags on the eve of the 1986 Masters. Those clubs certainly caught the attention of the USGA, who made the 3-Ball illegal or nonconforming right before that year's Masters started.

"The Wednesday afternoon before play began," Pelz recalls, "they posted a sign in the locker room that said, 'No Pelz Putters Allowed.'

"The putter failed to pass the written rule of golf, which states that a club must be 'plain in appearance,'" Pelz explains. Evidently the rule didn't apply to Jack Nicklaus's hugely oversized MacGregor Response putter, which the Golden Bear used to win the event. Sadly, Pelz's 3-Ball putter never saw the light of the green after that day until Odyssey Golf, a division of Callaway, licensed the patent from Pelz and brought out the 2-Ball putter at the 2002 PGA Merchandise Show in Orlando, Florida, as part of their White Hot putter series.

Intelligence may not help you play golf better, but it doesn't hurt when it comes to designing clubs. Larry Tang, an avid golfer and an amateur club designer working in the industrial design field in LA, became obsessed with Pelz's alignment-oriented idea.

"I read Pelz's book, *Putt like the Pros*," Tang says, "and became fascinated with his research, which showed how easily people can recognize objects that are identical in size and shape."

Now the rules of golf also state that a club can't be longer from front to back than it is wide from heel to toe, so when Tang set out in his garage to build a putter using balls as alignment aids, he decided he'd try two balls instead of three. This shortened the club lengthwise so that it would be within the rules. He had also learned from Pelz that it's the outline or silhouette of shapes, more than the shapes themselves, that people's brains register during the alignment act, so Tang dispensed with the balls and substituted white discs the exact diameter of golf balls in rigging up what would become the prototype of the 2-Ball putter.

As things turned out, Tang went to work for Odyssey just before Callaway bought it in 1997, and it didn't take long before he showed his 2-Ball prototype to Odyssey's top brass.

"I thought it looked funny when I first saw it," says Callaway's Dick Helmstetter, the company's former vice chairman and senior executive and now special consultant (and the man credited with inventing the original Big Bertha driver). "But after I stroked a few putts with it, I said, 'Wow,' and told Larry to go ahead and develop a few prototypes."

Callaway's former spokesman Larry Dorman pointed out that the company initially thought of using the putter in a prototype project to design and market extremely easy to hit golf clubs for absolute beginning golfers.

"So we brought in some pros to test these kinds of products," says Helmstetter. "We couldn't use absolute beginners to test these clubs, even though they were designed for them, because they have no consistency whatsoever in their swings.

"The pros loved the club so much we decided to mainstream it," Helmstetter concludes, and the rest is 2-Ball history.

Almost!

In 2006 Callaway's Odyssey Golf brought out a 3-Ball putter with an additional alignment disc, since new lightweight materials have allowed company designers to produce a rules-conforming club where length no longer exceeds width. Even in golf, everything goes around . . . and around . . . and around.

About Face

There's something about limits that gets our juices flowing. The closer we approach them, the more we want to test them. The more successfully we test them, the stronger our hunger grows to exceed and break them again. This is true everywhere in life, and especially with today's huge, thin-faced titanium drivers. The so-called "spring effect" of these clubs represents the greatest technological advancement the game of golf has seen perhaps since perimeter-weighted irons and putters appeared or since metalwoods themselves were introduced.

While thin-faced drivers occupy front and center stage in discussions of contemporary golf equipment, overlooked is the way they restore the long-lost pleasure of hitting a golf ball. People think that the appeal of those drivers lies solely in the added distance they produce (and they do hit the ball significantly farther than their oversized, plain-faced titanium predecessors). But big-headed sticks have also given drivers back their sweet spots.

Here's how. For the first time, advances in casting, forging, and metallurgy have allowed club makers to create titanium drivers with clubfaces that are slightly thicker at their centers than at their edges. Therefore, "thin-faced" refers to these clubs' peripheries and not actually to their centers. Strong, reinforced centers surrounded by weaker metal edges allow these clubs to function like small trampolines. Think about it: when a person jumps on a trampoline's center, that area must be strong enough to support his or her weight, while its edges should flex in order to rebound the jumper up into the air. Today's thin-faced drivers work the same way.

The clubs are manufactured with slightly stronger, thicker midsections, and their weaker edges allow these center portions to deform inwardly at impact. This "cupping action" results in a greater energy transfer between clubface and ball.

Think of throwing an apple out of a ten-story window. It would squash onto the pavement below. Were that apple to land on a trampoline, however, it would hardly compress at all; the flexing trampoline would rebound it back virtually whole into the air.

You can understand the excitement over the springlike effect in today's large-headed titanium drivers.

Just how well do these large thin-faced drivers perform? Some amateurs claim to hit them fifty yards farther than they did with their old steel drivers. Not too many years ago, Tour pros coveted drivers that hit the ball low and hit the ground running, but they can now launch their drives much higher into the air with these thin-faced clubs. Because they also produce less spin, the shots bore through the wind and still scoot forward like rabbits when they land.

Some equipment experts contend that these new clubs benefit only highly skilled golfers, who can generate clubhead speeds of at least a hundred miles per hour and consistently strike the ball in the center of the clubface. However, what's good for the goose is good for the gander; while slow-swinging hackers might not gain a lot more yardage with these new clubs, they will certainly hit the ball longer with them than they did before.

The founder of PING, Karsten Solheim, introduced the idea of "perimeter weighting" with his company's first putters and irons in the late 1960s. Then Gary Adams started TaylorMade and brought the first metalwoods to market. During the early 1990s, Ely Callaway combined Solheim's and Adams's ideas and developed the oversized Big Bertha driver. Callaway used stronger, lighter stainless steel, which allowed him to remove weight from the clubface's center and reposition it around its edges. This resulted in a very stable driver on off-center hits, but golfers paid the price for this on shots struck on the center (or sweet spot) of the club, which never felt completely solid. Manufacturers knew that few golfers hit the ball on the center of the clubface anyway, so they followed Callaway's lead and fortified the club's perimeter to yield improved shots on these expected poor swings.

A whole generation of golfers, whose grandparents were drawn to the game by the feel of solid impact with a persimmon driver, played for years without fully experiencing this inimitable sensation.

Today's drivers are so large, with heads measuring up to 460 centimeters in volume, that their designers must widen the clubfaces' solid center portions so they won't get lost in the expansive field of titanium that surrounds them. Now everyone can feel the satisfaction of centered impact, which may account for the growing popularity of the game among young people all around the world.

They used to say that more angels could dance on the head of a pin than on the sweet spot of a golf club, because the sweet spot of a club was so much smaller. Today that dance floor has expanded significantly. Ah, spring!!!

Vestigial Headcovers

They say titanium driver heads are virtually indestructible, and anyone who has clipped the leg of a coffee table with one, or dropped one on the concrete floor at a driving range, knows this is pretty much true. So why then do these clubs still come with headcovers? In years past, a cloth covering an old persimmon driver made a lot of sense. But there aren't that many persimmon drivers to be covered these days, and most golfers under the age of thirty probably have never even hit a ball with such a club.

The headcover is golf's vestigial organ, a piece of useless paraphernalia akin to our own tailbones, pointing to a primitive ancestry. It remains a mere souvenir of the game's past. Yet the driver headcover survives. Heck, it's thriving! Why?

Regardless of its utility or uselessness, it does sustain golf tradition, and old habits die hard. Within golfers' collective unconscious lives a healthy urge to yank off their drivers' headcover on the tee box before sizing up their impending shot.

Marketing offers another explanation. These boxing glove–sized wrappers blurt out the names of driver companies with the colorful unself-conscious teasing of Victoria's Secret ads on the sides of midtown Manhattan buses. That kind of promotion (of golf clubs, that is) harkens back to the early days of golf on television, when a new equipment company chose a name such as RAM because TV viewers could easily read the large letters on the side of a Tour bag. Today only the weary caddies of Tour pros tote such bulky luggage around the course, but the worst hackers' drivers sprout extravagant headcovers from Callaway, TaylorMade, Nike, or PING.

Golfers can hardly tell one of today's oversized titanium drivers from another, because they all are large, deep-faced, and black, and therefore carry no distinguishable status.

But a headcover—now, there's something to boast about! Some are painted in a rainbowlike manner that would make Jacob's coat look as bland as a jacket on the remainder rack at JCPenney. Some fasten onto their clubs via sexy zippers. "Benjamin, darling, can you come over here and unzip my R7 Quad?"

Some covers sport striped sleeves like those on a high school football team's jacket, which appeals to the wholesome soul of all athletes. Headcovers that bear no company name or logo use knitted woolen pompoms on top for a full-blown retro effect. One expects to find the handsome face of the late Tour pro and playboy Tony Lema pulling such a cover off the beautiful blond persimmon head of a Tony Penna driver (and if you're old enough to remember either Tony, then . . .).

Tiger Woods stands as the progenitor of the animal headcover craze. His stuffed-animal Tiger top functions as a triple reflexive sign: a tiger that identifies a headcover that can only belong to Tiger's driver. Images of school mascots on headcovers, such as a razorback hog, can link proud users to their hometown or state—John Daly and Arkansas. The headcover of a Badger may belong to Jerry Kelly, Andy North, Skip Kendall, Steve Stricker, or Sherri Steinhauer— Tour pros and Wisconsinites one and all. Or it could be mine, because I attended the University of Wisconsin.

While headcovers may no longer protect a driver head from nicks, scratches, mud, or moisture, they have survived to serve as security blankets under which macho metal clubheads can snuggle and take refuge from the lousy golf shots they hit. Even a good drive, hit miles ahead of one's playing partners, becomes a wayward sheep, and a lost sheep is an insecure one.

5

Golf and the Soul

The Golf Course as a Work of Art

"Rhythm must have meaning," poet Ezra Pound once said, and indeed rhythm forms the essence of poetry, art, and golf. So, in order to consider the golf course as a work of art, we first have to find the rhythm of the golf courses we love and play, and then look into the meaning of these rhythms. Now here I'm not talking about world-famous courses such as Pebble Beach, although, of course, who wouldn't enjoy a trip to the Louvre in Paris? I'm talking about any good golf course we love and play often and know intimately and well. I once asked legendary golf course architect Pete Dye what his favorite golf course was, and I assumed that he would understand I was asking about his favorite among all the world-famous courses he has designed. Instead he answered, "The little public golf course in Indiana I've been playing for years and years every Saturday with my buddies."

The Lido golf course on Long Island's South Shore in the town of Lido Beach is one of my favorite courses. The fact that it is a classic links style layout with some pedigree history to it only makes it that much more special. First designed by Charles B. Macdonald during the 1920s (who also designed and help build the first eighteen-hole golf course in the United States, the Chicago Golf Club), and then redone by another giant of golf course architecture, Robert Trent Jones Sr., in 1949, the course skirts Atlantic Bay and is serenaded by the fragrant sea breezes of the Atlantic Ocean located across the road.

A links course needs no long rows of trees to frame its holes or separate it from the outside world. Instead, its fairways slink low and seductive in front of you, as if they were mythical snakes illuminated with illicit knowledge carving paths over wet grass. So let's get on the first tee at Lido and listen hard to the music that the links course sings to us and to the golfing gods.

The first hole at Lido sounds a wide-open, long, and deep note, as if it were following a broad muscular paintbrush stroke. It begins the course's unfolding, the way a very familiar phrase the author purposely takes to the border of a cliché opens a novel. Hole 2 tightens considerably, with a lake on the left in range of a pulled tee shot, which instigates a subtle tightening of the belt and ignites that awful uneasiness we feel in our bodies while standing over certain golf shots. It's a fast reminder that hole 1's grandfatherly girth doesn't welcome us indefinitely—that any golf course can withdraw its love as rapidly as it gives it.

Number 3 narrows even more, with water left and right off the tee, water that acts as both the harbinger and enforcer of danger here and throughout the course. And this only reinforces the dreamy, unconscious quality of the links land itself. We remember that water in Jungian psychology symbolizes the unconscious, with its murky, fecund, and sometimes nightmarish depths. This apparently innocent, *childish*-looking golf course has percolating all around it the threatening penalty of death by drowning (of the golf ball, that is). Much of Lido's allure and charm comes from the perfectly balanced rhythm that this maze of lakes and the small inlets of the bay playfully establish as they dodge their way on and around the course's sandy soil. It's truly an erotic dance, as the water frames the golf course's land into a jagged painting, while the land holds the water's hand as it flows on in its devilish, carefree way.

The hole also instructs us on the theme of bravery. Though only 375 yards long from the back tees, it tests our capacity for straight-ahead focus and chivalrous resolve. Can we follow its morality-tinged "straight and narrow" path by directing our vision away from the long marsh flanking the right-hand side of the fairway, and an even smaller lake waiting like ball bait to gobble up any hooked or pulled drives down the left? The two bodies of water on this hole pinch the fairway's opposite sides into a slender waist, graceful and confident in its youthfulness.

This hole and holes like it stand as a refreshing chastisement of today's length-obsessed golf courses. It says that we who are modest of strength and mild in temperament may nevertheless summon up and depend on our courage to navigate through golf's and life's demands.

The idea of "the pause" plays a big part in establishing rhythm in any work of art. In painting, this pause often takes the form of a patch of canvas left untouched, around which the painter's images compose themselves in perfect balance and spacing, like white puffs of clouds on a summer's day. The caesura in poetry creates an almost imperceptible (though indispensable) pause in the middle of a poem, adding a bit of drama and delicious anticipatory tension to any verse via an almost unconscious registering of silence in the reader's ear—"What's going to come next?" Often the entire meaning of a line of verse balances itself on the sturdy nothingness of the caesura's acoustic break.

Hole number 4 at Lido fulfills this rhythmic function in that it exhales a long, straight, trouble-free corridor of fairway leading to a flat green. Here the artist takes his foot off of creativity's pedal just a little bit in preparation for the stunning sixth hole to follow. One of the two original holes remaining from Macdonald's original design, number six, sings a dizzying, disorienting song, which reminds me that golf and art's primary purpose is to captivate the soul and intoxicate the mind. Fashioned as a very sharp dogleg left (so much so that you can't see the green from the tee), the hole requires a lay-up drive short enough not to run out of fairway 230 or so yards away, but with enough get in its giddyup to carry 185 yards over a menacing patch of marsh directly in front of the tee box.

That the hole requires no more than a wedge to the green feels less worthy of mentioning than the transcendent power it has to transport golfers back to MacDonald's original design. The specters of golfers past play alongside those enjoying the game today. Even one hole like this, which stands as a vestige of a course long gone, consecrates the entire extended playing field and turns it into sacred ground.

Most great works of art have what we might call an "aesthetic center." In drama it's the play's denouement (the moment toward which the sum of the story's vectors and plots build and move). Paintings, sculptures, photographs, and prints also contain a specific point that draws the eye to them as if by a magnet. This kind of graphic gravity compresses the picture's power toward that spot, which makes the images revolve around it like winds encircling the eye of a storm.

Lido's other originally designed hole, the sixteenth, a 487-yard par five works beautifully this way. It generally plays much longer into predominant strong winds from the bay it faces, with two shots crossing water, as golfers must first carry a weedy mash in front of the tee that splits the fairway into left and right landing zones, like Robert Frost's two paths diverging in a wood. Golfers choosing the longer carry down the right side of the split fairway have slightly more than 200 additional yards to go over a large lake to the green, while the safer drive to the left landing area leads to a lay-up over the water and a pitch to the pin. It's tempting to say that the right fairway represents Frost's "the road less traveled by," and that taking it would "make all the difference" (which would allow us to play out the allusion to the poem to its fullest), but, truth be told, golfers gamble and play it safe in equal measure on this hole.

Hole 16 functions as Lido's emotional center. If the course were a play, here is where Laertes would murder Hamlet. If it were a portrait, it would have the glint in the eyes of Rembrandt's young son. This is the fertile and fecund darkness inside the bell of Miles Davis's trumpet. The 16th at Lido erupts and darts and weaves its way from tee to green with the agility of a Gale Sayers punt return. It's an impressive display of multiple planes that disorients and dazzles, emblazoning the entire course into a golfer's memory forever.

Many paintings incorporate images from ordinary life into their compositions. Some even use actual objects on their canvases, so that viewers find themselves scratching their heads trying to distinguish imagined from actual material. Even a nonmaterial art like poetry is not exempt from this reality-versus-illusion dialectic. Someone in the audience at a reading by the late poet Robert Creeley raised his hand and asked, "Is that a real poem, or did you just make it up?" Robert Rauschenberg's famous "combine paintings" paste real objects, such as paintbrushes, parts of beds, even a stuffed goat, directly onto the canvas. But a golf course, considered as a work of art, takes grass, bushes, flowers, sand bunkers, sky, trees, lakes, and shrubbery and utterly transforms them into a single expressive object.

A golf course presents a texture and surface all its own. For example, the soft, mushy fairways of Southern California's kikuyu grass fairways exude gentle innocence, like a baby's cheek, while the slick, firm bent grass greens of northern courses can overdo their authority, like the tight face of a highway patrol officer who pulls you over on his motorcycle.

A golf course considered as a work of art is like a chameleon that can shift its form at the drop of a headcover. Perhaps the versatile art of printmaking best captures this protean capacity. What other art-making process is capable of reproducing one basic image into subtly different colors and tones? In golf, instead of a variety of inks creating the different effects on each print, natural light acts as the medium. So a golf course in late September, with the reds and yellows and burnt ochres of autumn's leaves in fiery bloom, may offer a hearthlike warmth, while the golf course in winter, covered with snow, may turn a golfer's imagination inward in hibernation, storing energy as it does for the new season of play to come.

Great golf courses obviously cannot grace the galleries of museums but are themselves at times theaters of viewing for galleries of fans contemplating the game's best players. For example, A. W. Tillinghast's Winged Foot and Bethpage Black courses—both in New York State—hosted the 2006 and 2002 U.S. Opens, respectively (the U.S. Open returns to Bethpage Black in 2009), and both rank among the best golf courses in the entire world. Right next to the Black stands the Red course, a track I played countless times as a teenager in love with the game. I had the pleasure of reclaiming a bit of my lost youth not long ago when I teed it up on the Red again. This time I set my sights not just on where I wanted my golf ball to stop but also on the rhymes and rhythms, the structures and metaphors, of the course itself—on the golf course as a work of art.

Tillinghast's Red course feels like his Black's Siamese twin, siblings joined at the seams of their parallel first fairways. The Red, however, quickly darts north and insists on its own identity as a unique work of art. There's a linksy feeling here even though the course sits definitively inland. Since we're talking about Long Island, the allusion to links art—that is, to water—is as close as the Red's uniformly low trees, flat terrain, and wavy fescue grasses, not to mention the Atlantic Ocean, maybe five miles away.

The first hole at the Red carves a saddle-shaped landing area out of its elevated tees, which slides down into a wide, level, and low fairway. A 471-yard par four, this pretty painting demands the wholehearted involvement of a strong, long blast off the tee. The hole immediately involves the golfer as a character in the narrative the way a parent might nudge a child off the side of a swimming pool to shock her into independence. The impending demands of this hole seem to obliterate the normal first tee jitters, and after pounding a long iron or fairway metal up the hill to an elevated green, one's back has limbered and one's fighting mood feels fueled. It's a relief just completing this hole, but the respite is short-lived, as a storm of par fours bristle and brew not far ahead.

The Red course suddenly turns into a choreographer as the long, par five fifth pivots sharply to the right of the course's general flow before buttressing up against the tiny, short, par four sixth. Also a dogleg, this hole kinks sharply back to the left like a folded pinky. Together, this nimble duo outlines a zigzag pattern that guides golfers' feet over a green dance floor in a syncopated rhythm, like the spiraling embrace of proteins along DNA's entwined double axis.

But these dancers will soon turn monstrous, like any pair of feuding lovers, once the course reaches its midsection. There the playful roundness, like the paws of the petlike doglegs, so benign on the front side, gives way to a vicious parade of long par fours that roll forward with the force of a tsunami wave. Holes 9 and 10, for example—466-yard and 492-yard par fours, respectively—align themselves in opposite directions, like two runways at JFK. Hole 11 retrieves and repeats the dogleg motif, only with more calcium in its bones, clocking in at 432 yards. In the near distance lurks the 466-yard, par four fourteenth and the 482-yard, par four fifteenth, like a combination punch waiting to bring golfers to their knees, or like two contraindicated medications criminally prescribed by an overworked, distracted doctor.

Bethpage Red is the Big Canvas, the Rousing Symphony, the Tragic Play, where hubris, ambition, blind luck and, finally, fate lead each and every character/golfer to his or her salvation or demise.

Golf and Creativity

> Those little test pots are the way I get started. They're the best things I do. Everything I do is test pots so now there are no test pots.
>
> —Rudolf Staffel, noted ceramic artist

Amy Alcott is one of golf's all-time best players. She is also among the game's most articulate, intelligent, spirited, and creative champions. A World Golf Hall of Famer with twenty-nine victories, including five majors, Alcott burst onto the LPGA Tour directly out of high school in Pacific Palisades, California, and, unlike today's teenage prodigy Michele Wie, she did it without the aid of multiple multimillion-dollar endorsement deals. Amy's capital came in currencies of cunning, creativity, and a compact swing that allowed her to shape shots with a quality of imaginative and artistic contours that the golf world hasn't seen since the days of Ben Hogan, JoAnne Carner, and Lee Trevino.

It didn't surprise me when, years back, I learned while speaking with Amy at one of her tournaments that she painted too, just as Luke Donald of the European and American PGA Tours does. In her inimitably bold yet unassuming and gentle fashion, Amy would say in various interviews that she felt like an artist while she was playing golf. Until now, however, she hasn't talked at length about her painting in an interview.

However, I'm calling this piece an "intra-view," rather than an interview, because I want readers to get the sense of the spirited and, I hope, thought-provoking repartee of our conversation. I didn't so much want to ask Amy about golf and creativity as I wanted to *talk* with her about it.

There's a hit-and-miss quality to all creative acts in that what often at first appears to be an error or a mistake turns out to be some gem of wisdom—be it an instant insight about the golf swing or the random, beautiful way the glazes of a ceramic pot bleed together in the kiln. In this serendipitous spirit of following the curves of conversation, I sat down to speak with Amy Alcott about golf and creativity.

To begin with, I was really curious about what Amy meant when she described a golfer as an artist, and herself as an artist when she plays golf. Could it be something about the golf club being like a paintbrush (after all, both create "strokes") or about the course as a canvas? Amy's response cut more directly to the soul of what being an artist is all about.

Here's what she had to say: "I think while each person is different, among all great and exceptional players there is a very calm, focused, Zenlike quality that allows them to get in the zone. And then I think there is a more manic, insecure side to them, a swashbuckling side, for lack of a better term, and the great players have a rare blending of both sides."

I myself knew the Zen type well, as it has become the metaphor of choice for many who love golf and who search for a way of expressing the inexpressible essence of the game. But that there could be utilitarian golf value to a manic personality surprised me, so I asked Amy to explain.

"Well, I think there's a go-for-broke attitude among great players, a not-to-settle-for-the-mundane side of things, that makes them want to challenge things and go for things. I think of an artist like a Jackson Pollock, who would go out there and be creative, versus somebody who just draws between the lines."

Of course, Pollock's dripped and thrown paintings did break free, as Amy said, from any sense of confinement, moving art in a new direction of self-expression.

"Right," she answered after my observation, "and I think great golfers are complicated like great artists. And I think how amazing it would be if Nicklaus and Palmer were melded into one person. You have the great Germanic, tactician, statistician methodical type, like Nicklaus, and then you have the Arnold Palmer 'grip it and rip it' type. Both are artists in their own way."

I couldn't help mentioning Nietzsche's division of artists into the Apollonian and Dionysian archetypes, with the first being the one who reasons out where his or her work of art is going before starting it. Such an artist executes the work of art as if following a blueprint or plan, the way Jack Nicklaus would manage his game so precisely around the toughest of golf courses. The Dionysian/Palmer type of artist follows a wilder, intoxicating, and spontaneous path of creativity. He or she intuitively makes the work of art, or the round of golf, up as he or she goes along.

Maybe Tiger Woods combined a little bit of both types of artist in his golf game and soul, I suggested.

"Well, maybe so," Amy mused, "and there are probably others who are struggling to find a balance."

I wanted us to speak about Amy, so I asked her, "How is the game of golf creative for you?"

"When I was in a certain state of mind and my swing was under control," she answered, "I would stand at the back of the driving range in a little fairway-like practice area between holes 1 and 2 at Riviera Country Club with my teacher Walter Keller, and we'd hit shots. I'd have to hit sweeping fades, and sweeping draws and punch shots, and after a while, he would just sit and watch, because he knew he wouldn't have to tell me what to do. He enjoyed seeing that my interest and desire to be creative and play shots was there."

"My problem with golf as it's played now," she continued, "is that it's kind of boring. Because of the new equipment, you don't have to be a shot maker or an artist. There's just a lack of creativity, though you do still see some creativity around the greens."

I agreed that the only discussion you hear nowadays regarding a player's creativity seems to limit itself to the short game. I pointed out that when Amy and I were growing up, however, creative players, such as Chi Chi Rodriguez, Lee Trevino, Seve Ballesteros, Gary Player, and others, were capable of shaping and inventing shots *from tee to green.*

"Yeah, right," she chimed in, "back in those days, we had heavier steel shafts, but when the lighter graphite shafts came around, the good players complained that they couldn't control the ball and play different shots. Now the heads are so big and the balls have less spin, and it's harder to be creative."

"But as far as the artistic side of golf," she continued, "I think I always just enjoyed being creative because I get bored quickly. If I had a teacher who said, 'Always hit me a shot with a fade,' that would have squelched my creativity, and I would have never been the player I was. In golf, you really never have the same shot twice, so you had better be prepared to hit different shots. And if you're creative, and you enjoy practicing, which is like working on your pen-and-paper drawings down on the driving range, then you're more prepared when you have to hit the shots creatively in competition."

I wanted to bring the conversation from the realm of practice into one of competition, so I asked Amy to recall some of the more creative shots she played on her way to the Hall of Fame.

"I can remember playing this shot at Mission Hills during the 1983 Nabisco Dinah Shore back from behind some trees the first year I won that tournament. It was a big sweeping hook with a six iron, and I've gone back to that spot. To this day, I can't remember how I played such a great shot. I knocked it on the green and two putted, which let me go on to win the tournament."

Then an even more excited tone crept into Amy's voice.

"For another one of my Nabisco wins in '88 I remember playing the eighteenth hole in one of those desert wind storms. I drove it off the tee into the rough and had to hack a seven wood up the fairway. That left me way, way back, with a shot to the green into a strong wind. We got up to the ball, and I had a one-stroke lead and a 170-yard shot to the front edge of the green dead into the wind.

"My caddie was nervous. He said, 'Let's just lay up.' So I said to him, 'I'm going to have to teach you how to win.' Then he said again, 'But if you go for it with that three iron you're trying to play, and you miss-hit it or something, you could lose the tournament by making a seven.' He's talking to me like this in the fairway. So again I said, 'Well, I need to show you how to win.' I told him it was live by the sword or die by the sword. We were either going to hit the good shot and win this tournament with style, the way I can win it, or we go down with the count."

"So what did you do?" I asked Amy.

"I hit an incredible hooked three iron with so much spin and juice on it!" she exclaimed. "And it just barely carried the water by three feet and got up on the green. I two putted and won. It was a stupid shot and it was incredibly marginal, but I knew I had enough of a chance and enough adrenaline to do it. A lot of golf and, I suppose, life is being able to look yourself in the mirror and say, 'I did it my way.'"

I was breathless just listening to this, and it made me want to get back to the solitude of the practice tee. So I asked Amy if she recommended that people practice in the creative way she outlined a bit earlier.

"When I do clinics, I have people work on shots of different distances, and never have them hit the same shot twice. I give them a thirty-, fifty-, and seventy-yard shot, and they can't go back and say, 'Woops, I misjudged that one, I'm going to hit it over again.' I tell people, 'In golf you never have the same shot twice.' Sure, you can stand there with a bag of balls and hit a hundred balls at the fifty-yard marker, but what the hell are you doing? You're just getting exercise. By varying your shots, you're practicing. You get more mentally exhausted, but at least you are practicing."

I asked Amy if she found a specific correlation between making a painting and playing golf.

"There's a freedom to painting that makes me feel like I'm inside the ropes, as when I'm playing in a golf tournament," she said.

"And that's exactly where I have to be. I was kind of born to be inside the ropes."

So it was the sense of immersion or flow in the activity of playing golf and painting that appealed to her.

"Yes, I like being active and, probably, in control, and feeling that I'm the creator of my own destiny. But there is also a part of painting and golf to me that is very reclusive. You have to be ok with being a very solitary and self-motivated person. Like all those years nobody ever saw me hitting balls six hours a day by myself."

Speaking with Amy about golf and art was like dying and going to heaven. There are no bad shots, really, when you are having such a stimulating conversation. There was none of the frustration of playing golf—or writing, for that matter—attached to our conversation either, and I wished the talk would go on forever. However, I had promised her we'd keep the session to forty-five minutes, and that time frame was narrowing. I needed to get to a topic we hadn't yet broached: the golf course as a work of art. I wanted to find out if she shared my view that a course was indeed a work of art.

"Of course, and I find it interesting how at tournament courses, if you are there on Sunday night after the people leave, you can still hear the echoes of the yelling and the clapping from a birdie or a great shot. A golf course is an amazing arena on which people can showcase their talent. And when no one is around, that's when a golf course is the most beautiful to me—when it's quiet and there's not a soul there.

"It's the quiet and the sprinklers that really get to me. It's going out to Riviera at 4:30 in the afternoon, with the course's incredible shades of green in and out of the shadows, and throwing a couple of clubs in my bag and walking down the fairway, and have somebody drive by and say, 'Well, what are you doing out here by yourself?' They look at me like 'You're a Hall of Famer, there are only fifteen of you women in the Hall, and you're out here by yourself?'"

You mean, they're like, "Why are you enjoying yourself like this as if you were just another golfer?" I asked.

"Right. But I realize that as much as things change, they also stay the same. In those moments, I'm going back in time to when I was ten years old. There's not much of me that's changed, because I still really love the game so much. It's a very personal thing to me."

Nothing had ever seemed more obvious—or more heart-warming.

Golf and Spirituality

If my piece with Amy Alcott was an "intra-View," I'm obliged to call this one an "intra-*review*," because it's a talk with the inimitable Michael Murphy about his book *Golf in the Kingdom*. Michael founded the education and research center Esalen Institute in Big Sur, California, and is recognized as one of the founding fathers of the human potential movement in the United States, which blends Eastern and Western philosophy in a variety of disciplines and everyday walks of life. His first book, *Golf in the Kingdom*, is a marvelous bible of golf and spirituality.

I had taken copious notes, each reflecting my best effort to perceive the metaphorical signs of transcendence blended into the story of the narrator, Michael, who, while on his way to India to study with a guru, finds first enlightenment through his friendship with a fictitious Scottish golf pro, Shivas Irons, in the imaginary Scottish town of Burningbush.

I might have waited to see the movie, whose rights Clint Eastwood has owned for years, but the film has yet to be made. I might have Ti-Voed Peter Jacobsen's wonderful golf show, *Peter Jacobsen Unplugged*, which aired on the Golf Channel, since as much as any golfer I know of today, Peter embodies the creative and playful spirit of Shivas, but I don't have TiVo. So I was stuck with my often unreadable scribble of notes, a sprawling mass of ragged notebooks compiled with a dumb cup of coffee next to me in Starbucks and in the margins of the book itself, so dog-eared now I've renamed my copy "Spot."

But a round of golf never unfolds as one imagines, and neither does a piece of writing worth its weight in printer cartridges. Taking notes for an interview is like warming up on the driving range before a round of golf, as each initiates a flowing of ideas and movement in the brain and the body. After hitting balls I can step onto the first

tee with the apparatus for shot making well oiled; after taking notes
I can face the snowy tablet of the blank page with a little less fear.

But I already knew in my heart of hearts the question with which
I wanted to begin my talk with Michael Murphy: "Does the expression 'When you meet the guru on the path, kill him' have any relevance to golf or to your book *Golf in the Kingdom* in particular?"

Now I view and experience golf as a creative activity by which one
can discover more about one's essential nature as well as express
something vital about one's soul. In other words, golf is an inward
thing for me. However, there is so much today about the game that
draws us away from our centers, and one of those nefarious mag-
nets comes in the form of golf's big-time celebrity instructors, who
present themselves as knowing all of the answers. Those instructors
benefit financially by setting themselves up as "gurus," or ultimate
authorities, while we mere mortals, who know nothing, must sub-
mit ourselves (and our credit cards) to their wisdom.

"If you meet the guru on the path, kill him" suggests that if someone claims to have this kind of power over you, he or she must be an
impostor, because the answers that we seek lie within. Since *Golf in
the Kingdom* tells a story about the narrator (Michael Murphy acknowledges him as himself), who finds enlightenment through the
golf/spiritual teacher Shivas Irons, I wanted to begin our discussion
of the book with an exploration of this quote.

Michael paused distinctly, sizing up both the question and me.
Then, with patience extracted, it seemed, from the very book under review, he spoke.

"You know, any kind of instruction in any field is invaluable. But
as you achieve mastery, or at least as you improve, you have to be
sure that the instruction you seek and receive is adapted to your native talents and to your soul's appetites and tendencies. I think the
principle holds in every aspect of life. We don't become human without loving-kindness and care, and this is well demonstrated in studies of feral children. Now one can learn golf by mimicry—that is to
say, by copying accomplished others—or by learning the basic fun-

damentals. Then one has to practice, because, as they say, 'practice makes perfect,' but only if it's the right kind of practice. Practicing things that are wrong for you only ingrains bad habits."

Michael seemed to be warming up and gaining momentum as he spoke, and this pleased (and relieved) me, since he could have been offended by the abruptness of my question. But his answer was full of the very sort of loving-kindness of which he spoke. In other words, I saw that I should be careful of categorical definitions or explanations, even, if not especially, of such clichéd slogans as "When you meet the guru on the path, kill him." So there I was, awakened to a new interpretation of the saying, when I had rigidly believed there was only one.

"Now some people, like Hogan and Tiger, are natural geniuses on the mental side of the game," Michael continued. "Whereas others with tremendous physical skills don't have as much hold on the mental side of golf, and they can use a sport psychologist or one of these new teachers of the inner game."

Certainly no book has embraced the inner game with as much charm and literary acumen as Michael's, which has, since its publication in 1972, sold over a million copies in many different languages. It has become the standard against which all other books on golf and spirituality have tried—and, in my opinion, failed—to reach.

I was curious how he came to write the book in the first place.

"In a very real sense, it wrote itself," Murphy began. "It was the first book I ever wrote, and the first book I even tried to write, and by the time it was published I was forty-one. I had had the idea in my head for a while of writing about meeting this shaman, this mystic, on the golf course, but I didn't have a set theme. I was trying to dramatize the fact that all of life, and all of our activities in life, including playing golf, can become the venues for the expression of supernormal powers and of illuminations."

Was he referring to the scene in which Shivas takes Michael out to the course in the middle of the night? There, with his ego metaphorically obscured by the darkness, Michael learns from Shivas to swing from the center of his being (what Shivas calls "the inner body"), and this allows him to hit the ball better than he ever has before.

In addition to its wisdom, there is a tremendous amount of humor in the book, particularly in section 2, where Michael discusses golf in spirited and poetic ways. More prosaic golfers may call a tee shot on a par three that finds the bottom of the hole an "ace," but Shivas Irons sees it as a "Galactic-Ecstatic-Hole-in-One." There is also a cataloglike string of metaphors for the golf ball, which include "a smaller waffled version of the crystal ball; an old stone to polarize your psyche with; a satellite revolving around our higher self; a reminder of our hunting history and our future powers of astral flight; and an egg laid by man."

"I was consciously going over the top at times, particularly in section 2," Michael conceded, "because to get so serious about something so patently absurd as the game of golf really does invite laughter."

It has always amazed me, seriously, that when you ask people what it is they want from the game, only a few will answer, "I want lower scores." Most either say they want to hit the ball farther or play more consistently. I've *never* heard of anyone saying, "I want to play by the rules," even though it is only because golf *has* rules that it even qualifies as a game. Yet on page 20, Shivas tells Michael that playing by the rules "is the only way ye can play in the kingdom."

I just assumed that the "kingdom" meant "the inner kingdom." "I don't know if 'the kingdom' is inner," Michael cautioned. "It's inner *and* outer. The implication is that the kingdom is the Kingdom of Heaven, and that's the double entendre of the title. *Golf in the Kingdom* is at once the Kingdom of Fife and the Kingdom of Heaven. About the Kingdom of Heaven, Jesus says, 'I've come not to break the law, but to *fulfill* it.'"

"One of the great beauties of golf is its obsession with the rules," Michael continued. "There's no other game that has devoted so much time, energy, or money to its rules. Every ten years or so, the USGA does an updating of the rules, which it coordinates with the Royal and Ancient in Scotland. They spend well over a couple of million dollars of pro bono time from lawyers meditating on such minutiae as 'when a ball comes on the fly into the club, embeds itself under the lip, but doesn't make it to the bottom of the cup, is that ball holed out or not?' The answer is no. The ball has to reach the bottom of the cup. All of this time and energy and money spent on the rules is a sign of the wonderful devotion to the game and the code of honor that envelops it."

Michael then revealed himself as a true sports fan by saying that "in football, there is a whole different ethic of getting away with as much holding as you can. If you're an interior lineman, one of your methods is to learn to hide your holding from the referee. Golfers, on the other hand, have called penalties on themselves that have caused them to lose tournaments."

I brought up the situation at the LPGA Tournament at Big Horn in the California desert at the end of the 2005 season, where a golf writer pointed out to a rules official that Michele Wie had committed a rules violation. I've always felt that someone outside of the official competition itself (i.e., the golf tournament) shouldn't be allowed to participate in administering the rules of the game.

But Michael said, "It happens all the time at baseball games where the fans yell and wildly prompt the umpires: 'He was out, ump! You're blind!' I've been down on the sidelines of football games where the coaches and the water boys are shouting at the referees constantly."

To me, though, what makes a game a game is that its playing field sets the action off from the rest of the world in a virtual space, and those not within the ropes, so to speak, can watch, enjoy, cheer, and have opinions about the rulings but they can't become part of the actual competition. People argue that the law is the law and that the method with which someone brings an athlete's breaking of the rules to the officials' attention doesn't matter. I think it does, because we are talking about the rules of a game, and not about a society's laws. Because a game provides *relief* from the spectators' everyday life, all aspects of the game should remain, in a sense, sacredly segregated from quotidian reality. Sport, like art, is an *imagined* reality. No one would call the New York City Police and tell them that Othello is about to murder his wife, Desdemona, during a performance of Shakespeare's play in Central Park. In my opinion, the golf writer should have been excluded from Michele Wie's drama as well.

"This is why we have moral philosophy, which is what you are practicing here," Michael, ever patient with my protracted analogies, said. "And moral philosophy is not mysticism [by which he meant that it doesn't deal with the ultimate big questions about our existence] but it is important on the way to the pure, the good, and the beautiful life."

I wanted to get back to the idea of the Kingdom of Play. Jesus also said we should become as children again, I pointed out, and then asked Michael if he had ever seen a child with an overly mechanical golf swing.

He answered no and then, veering away from Christianity, he one-upped me in scholarship by reminding me that Nietzsche said, "There is no one that is more serious than a child at play."

I came back with a quote from Antonio Machado, Spain's greatest poet of the last century, who said, "Art was intense play." Michael agreed.

Although Shivas Irons believes adhering to the rules of golf to be a spiritual thing, he also tells Michael, "Don't worry about the score."

I wondered if this wasn't a bit of a paradox, because don't the rules themselves determine the way in which a golfer arrives at his or her score?

"I always say that a person's relation to paradox is a measure of their enlightenment," Michael responded.

Then I told Michael that I related only too well to the narrator of his book, who, after making a ten-on-one hole, listens to Shivas tell him, "I think it was an eleven, Michael." So much of *Golf in the Kingdom* also has to do with the game forcing people to both face and subdue their egos.

"You're a very good reader," the real Michael said, massaging my ego. He went on to say that "part of mastery is to be wholehearted and focused and intense in what you are doing, and to do it with as much equanimity and internal freedom as possible, which are attributes that can be cultivated. You can be focused and intense and yet unflappable in the face of a shank. That's why Ben Hogan had that powerful, magnetic, and deep presence about him: he practiced all the time."

When he mentioned Hogan and practice, I wanted Michael's opinion about Hogan's saying that golf's "secret is in the dirt: go and dig it out of the dirt." I've always believed Hogan was talking not only about practice but of golf as a ritualized act of tearing of the earth, like the orgiastic Dionysian rite of tearing the grape to make wine. The divot, I always felt, was like a pagan vegetable god that signified the cycle of planting, growing, and harvesting, and whose rebirth presaged Christ's return from the dead.

"That's a nice reading of Hogan's saying," Michael said graciously. "That may have been Hogan's unconscious wisdom or poetry coming out, but he was also obviously referring to just hitting golf balls."

I told Michael that I thought a *Golf in the Kingdom* instruction book, which could teach people to play via such gems of wisdom as "the ball and the club are joined before the golfer swings" would both make for fabulous reading and help golfers play better.

All he said to me was, "I ain't gonna write it."

Michael never becomes overly explicit or heavy-handed in the novel, which is one of its major accomplishments. For example, he never actually links the name *Shivas* with the Hindu god of destruction and renewal, Shiva, even though many readers know well of Murphy's involvement in Eastern thought. He simply lets the readers make the connection for themselves.

"When I wrote the book, I had not named him, but then I started a search through all the Scottish clan names, and I found both Shivas and Irons, and two years later, after the publication of the book, Tiger Woods was born. So here you have irons and woods, and soon some mysterious character will emerge, 'Billy Joe Putter.' Then we'll have a complete set of clubs, with this threesome of Shivas Irons, Tiger Woods and Billy Joe Putter."

I laughed.

Of course, the full magic allure of *Golf in the Kingdom* lies in the fact that Michael, the narrator, gains both spiritual enlightenment *and* improves his golf game through the guidance of Shivas Irons, while the "actual" guru he was traveling to study with in India becomes a mere afterthought.

Michael Murphy says, "We're given these graces, and we turn our back on them and walk away all the time *even though they are staring us right in the face.* That's the supreme irony and ultimate lesson of the book. The world is always there offered to us, and we, in our blindness, even when we *think* we are headed toward enlightenment, aren't able to or don't turn to the grace that is given to us."

I felt a kind of thematic gravity (or stubbornness?) pulling me back to the starting point of our conversation, so I thought I'd take another crack at "The Question." So I tried again. "Doesn't the expression, 'When you meet the guru on the path, kill him,' suggest that we shouldn't project power or ultimate authority onto anyone, or any institution, outside of ourselves who appears and/or *pretends* to have all the answers about our lives?"

Michael, somehow still incredibly patient, responded by saying, "Well, that's really much more of a Western sentiment," and though he tossed off the thought like someone slipping out of his or her slippers at bedtime, it felt like the answer I had been looking for all these years. It's wasn't the imbalance of power in the dynamic relationship of two people that had obsessed me; it was the whole Western imbalance of seeing everything in terms of a dualistic competition—Man versus Nature, Us versus Them, Teacher versus Student, Subject versus Object.

"The greatest teachers are those who foster the unique enlightenment of the disciple, and it's always been thus," Michael went on, perhaps more pensive now that at any other time during our talk so far. "Yet authoritarian relationships do develop, which are called 'cults,' and then the whole relationship between the teacher and the student can become monstrous."

I was getting what I wanted here, and while I was aware that I might be taking golf a little too seriously, I blurted out anyway, "And the same thing happens with a lot of the golf instruction gurus."

"Well, that's right," he answered, "there are golf teachers who wrongly try to fit all of their students into cookie cutter swings," meaning one formulaic swing of which they are the sole source and the supreme administrators.

"That can happen," he continued, "and it can happen with all kinds of teachings. But, again, it's complex. Adlai Stevenson once said, 'We have to have the courage of our *insincerity*,' meaning, you have to practice 'as if,' and then pretty soon, by god, you internalize the teaching you have received. So in golf, you would get up there and swing and you hit the ball where you're aiming, and before you know it you're doing it more consistently.

"Every time you set out to write a book, how the hell do you know you can actually finish this book, or that it will be any good? So we are always stretching out beyond ourselves and living 'as if.' Think about the courage of starting a sentence. Do you know that I have not the faintest thought at all of how I'm going to finish this sentence? But I just finished it there! You see?"

"It's a leap," I interjected.

"It's one of the great mysteries of speech, that we can say the most elaborate, most labyrinthine, the most curlicue, the most meandering sentence, and it ends up—bing! with a period. Just like that! You know, I didn't rehearse that!"

"That was good, too," I said quickly.

"This is how you and I go through life," Michael continued. "We are improvising every instant. And that involves a lot of 'as if's. In other words, what starts out feeling artificial becomes more and more spontaneous the more you practice, like, say, dancing. Anyone of us who has tried to learn the salsa, or the tango, or whatever, understands. At first you're very stilted, and, by gosh, the next thing you know, it's second nature! So finding a richer, freer enjoyment playing golf involves assuming a certain attitude. The Buddhist said, 'The eight-fold noble path begins with right attitude.' If someone's got bad attitude, they are going to be an unwholesome presence. A *good* attitude is needed!"

I felt myself becoming not a disciple, actually, but a transfixed and mesmerized listener.

The student-teacher relationship takes an interesting turn in *Golf in the Kingdom* when Shivas asks Michael to be his voice and to communicate his wisdom out into the world. I was curious if Michael intended Shivas and Michael to be symbols of the inner and outer worlds, respectively.

"Well, that's a wonderful reading!" Michael exclaimed, "but this whole notion that Shivas Irons is a figure of the Soul in us wasn't anything I had in mind when I set out to write the book. Rather, what I did have in mind was the classic German Bildungsroman form, which is a character-building novel, a quest novel, which involves the young lad and the teacher."

"But you can read the character of the teacher in a Bildungsroman novel as the image of the projected figure of the Soul itself," I said.

"In that case," Michael answered, "the idea of Shivas as the Soul that Michael summons into existence in the outside world is a very good understanding. Sometimes the reader sees things in the work that the writer doesn't."

I felt rather pleased with myself, which is probably why, at that particular moment, I recalled the expression "It is a poor student who in some ways does not excel the teacher." In what ways, I wondered out loud, had Michael excelled Shivas Irons?

"So far he hasn't," Michael replied, laughing. But that didn't sound right to me.

"Michael was the one who wrote this fantastic book," I pointed out.

"Good work again!" Michael said.

Then he signaled the imminent end of our conversation by initiating a discussion of what he called "the journey round archetype." Through the journey round we come to understand our lives as if seen for the first time with new eyes.

"The image of the 'journey round,'" Michael said, "is the combining of the two great sets of symbols of eternity." He explained that the linear one out of the Judeo-Christian tradition imagines time as progressing in a cause-and-effect, A-to-B-to-C-to-D fashion. The circular ones of Eastern and Ancient Greek thought, Michael said, posit that "the world isn't going anywhere, and that we can merge with being itself."

He added, "The philosopher and theologian Paul Tillich told us all at the end of his life that the great task in the decades ahead would be to merge the two great sets of symbols, the linear and the circular."

I pointed out that we're all trying to hit a golf ball straight with a circular swing.

"There's another connection that never occurred to me!" Michael said enthusiastically, and though he wasn't trying to, he had bolstered my confidence in my ideas about his wonderful novel. Perhaps, I thought after we parted ways, we all do need a true guru or two to help us clarify our beliefs and convictions. I just wish more were like Michael Murphy.

Bob'n Around

I play a lot of golf with Robby Krieger—guitarist and songwriter for the Doors, the sweet-swinging and now khaki pants–wearing genius who penned "Light My Fire" and other hits of that great group—so I'm not deprived in the rock-star-turned-golf-nut playing partner category. But after learning recently that Bob Dylan played golf, I thought I'd rather tee it up with him than with anybody in the world; after all, my first poetry teacher, Marilyn Kallet, said he was "God." Sure, I'd enjoy a round with Jack or Arnie or Tiger or Gary Player—well, Gary *is* golf's greatest philosopher-poet, so that might be a tough choice. But if Dylan *is* God, then he's my guy for a Saturday game.

Of course, the odds on my reserving the twosome of Bob Dylan and me are about as good as my spending the day on the links with the real God, assuming it turns out that Bob *isn't* him. This is to say, my chances are slim and none—and Slim left town last week.

So all that's left is to *imagine* playing a game of golf with the great one, whose lyrics sound loosened from the tongue of an angel and whose voice seems strained through a Zen garden of gravel. So I booked the tee time in my mind with Bob Dylan himself!

"Hey Bob, come on, man, you're pretty late! Our tee time is in ten minutes. Don't you want to hit some balls?"

"Sorry, he answered, "Traffic was murder *out there on Highway 61,* and I ain't talkin' figuratively; there was some cat out there callin' himself Abraham, who said God was telling him *to kill me a son,*" or some such nonsense.

"Forget about it, dude," I replied, "that's like way too heavy for me at 6:30 in the morning!"

"You're right," Bob agreed; then he exclaimed that early morning was "*the time I love the best!*" and that it wasn't good karma to begin the day with a violent thought or image.

I chimed in, "Right on!" then stared at Bob's way-cool golf shoes as he laced them up on the bumper of his gold Lexus suv.

"Bobby, you got some wicked Soft Spikes there."

"Yeah," he said, though a little sadly, I thought, "they're *Spanish boots of Spanish leather*." The story was that an ex-love of his sent them to him from Spain, as a kind of farewell gift, meaning she didn't want to see him anymore.

But it seemed he wanted to win her back by using his contacts in the golf industry to sell the idea of these golf boots to Footjoy or Nike as a "concept shoe," he called it, and that would impress her. But it didn't work.

For some reason he chose to tell me about the negotiation process with the shoe company.

"First of all they kept calling me '*Tambourine Man*,' as if that had anything to do with golf shoes. Worse was they paid it no mind when I demanded a little respect by saying, 'It's *Mister Tambourine Man*.' The manager of one of those golf shoe companies explained that while they liked the concept for the Spanish golf boots, they would be too hot on the feet to go over well in big markets like Arizona, Palm Springs, and Florida."

Then Bob turned inward, as if thinking, before musing, "Ya know, I never went over real big in those markets, either."

But an unexpected visitor meant that all hope wasn't lost.

A skinny guy, young, but still too old in my opinion to be wearing a Green Day T-shirt, appeared out of nowhere and said, "Hey Bob, I work for Footjoy, so if you're heading up to *the North Country*, you know, *where the wind blows heavy on the borderline* with Canada [Suddenly, I felt like I was the one straddling some thin divide between sanity and its beyond, because I kept hearing—or should I say 'hearin'?—everything that Bob was asayin' as words from his songs!], stop in and see our Minnesota rep. People play golf in all kinds of slush and slop up there. And while you're in the region, please look up Stina Stevenson and say hi for me, because "*she once was a true love of mine*."

Whatever.

I didn't appreciate the intrusion, and I feared that people would keep coming up to Bob all day long and that it would ruin our round of golf, so I tried to redirect his attention back to me with a little joke.

"These boots were made for walkin'," I said, then winced, because I thought the comparison with Nancy Sinatra and her dumb '60s song would send the bard back out on Highway 61 heading for home. But he just sort of chuckled, you know, with a little forgiving growling sound, like a satisfied cat, and said, "*Don't think twice*," about it, "*it's alright.*"

It was time to play and, as we stood on the first tee, there was no way I wouldn't give my one and only hero the honors.

I said, "Play away, Bobby!"

He shot me a quick, "What's up with that?" sort of look, to which I responded, "Nobody's ever called you that before?" But I wasn't looking for any friction here and figured these celebrity types are used to everybody kissing their skinny behinds and it might do Bob some good to spend a little time with ordinary nobodies like me.

It was a cool autumn day, breezy too, and while he was making some practice swings (yes, Bob Dylan takes practice swings!), I sank into my own nonmusical golf world by tossing up some blades of grass into the air to check the condition of the breeze.

I just *knew* it was coming, and Bob didn't skip a beat, when he said, "Look, bro', *you don't need a weatherman to know which way the wind blows.*"

"To coin a phase," I retorted, not wanting to be taken for an illiterate dope.

But Dylan had already started to swing, frankly a very stiff-looking action, though not without a degree of talent latent in it. In fact, more than anyone's, Bob's motion reminded me of Calvin Peete's—remember him, a great African American golfer during the 1980s and one of the game's straightest drivers and most underrated ball strikers ever?

Calvin has some sort of degenerative left arm that he can't fully straighten, so his swing sort of wobbled and looped back and up and then down and in, and so did Bob's. But Bob nevertheless unleashed a tremendous blow into the ball, which flung the head of his Big Bertha driver right off its shaft.

"*She breaks just like a little girl,*" he said, shaking his head. Then he showed me that he was in fact a true golfer, a "golfer's golfer," as my friend the late Gary Adams, founder of TaylorMade Golf, used to call people who played the game with their soul on their sleeve and weren't afraid to show their frustration, because he said, "*I do believe it's time for us to quit.*"

Actually, at first I thought he said, "It's time for *me* to quit," which aroused some sympathy in me for my fellow suffering golfer and new friend, but when I realized he actually quoted his own song and said, "*It's time for us to quit,*" I got mad.

"Damn it, Bob, I get to play maybe once a month if I'm lucky [it's completely untrue that golf writers like me or others who work in the golf industry play all the time!], and I haven't even teed-off yet, so, relax, baby!"

"Don't worry," I comforted him, "you'll get better! And send that Big Bertha head and shaft back to Callaway. They're great about repairing or replacing clubs that break like yours at no charge."

We were both taking too much time on the first tee, and Tony Wise, the course's head pro, known for his almost fascistic strict tactics to move play along, strode up to us.

"Step it up, boys, you're not the only people who want to finish before dark today. And Bob, tuck your shirt in, man!"

This upset Bob, who, as my guest, wanted to maintain a polite demeanor, but it seemed he just couldn't contain himself, because he glared at me, shook his head, and mumbled in his characteristically nasal voice, "*Don't follow leaders who watch the parking meters.*"

This cryptic figure of speech caught me off guard, though I laughed, delighted as I was by the simple rhyme of "leaders" and "meters." Thankfully, Tony had turned his weather-beaten face away and started to look for other members to harass with his militaristic style of country club management and hadn't heard Bob's somewhat spirited slogan.

Yet all the same, I felt in my Gary Adams golfer's soul that Tony had a point and that while slow play on any golf course is of course completely infuriating, it also presents an opportunity to practice patience. I reminded myself of the age-old cliché that "a bad day on the golf course is better than a good day at the office." In fact, I was about to share that bit of white-collar proletarian wisdom with Bob, but I bit my tongue, because, first, that's not really very cheerful encouragement, and, second, the image of Bob Dylan working in an office struck me as bizarre, if not surreal.

Bob evidently read my mind, because he corrected me by saying, "My line about the parking meters is a metaphor; it ain't surrealism, you idiot. It means don't live by other people's rules, especially fuckin' uptight golf pros."

Even so, we obediently started walking down the first fairway at a brisk pace, which made it difficult for both of us to follow golf's number one rule: relax and play your own game.

By the fourth hole, however, Bob had begun to strike the ball beautifully, and if you can believe it, he was one under par at that point! Those small heels on his Spanish golf boots, though they might have looked more in place at a Greenwich Village coffeehouse, were getting the job done. They were allowing his spry frame to pivot like a hurricane through the ball, with as much authority as Ben Hogan.

"You ever think of turning pro?" I asked him on the fifth tee. I did so cautiously, because as his answer would indicate, it was not a possibility anyone even mildly respectful of the heart-and-soul demands of being a poet would have ever dreamed of raising.

"I'm not Kenny G!" he retorted, with a kind of James Dean, teen-agelike rebellious anger, and a bit more venom than I felt comfortable absorbing.

"I never said you were," I answered defensively, and I wasn't sure if by that he meant that he felt his swing was superior to the highly praised one of the moderately praised saxophonist or that he didn't entertain unrealistic fantasies about his game. In either case, I saw no value whatsoever in putting Kenny G further down, so I left it at that—well, almost at that, because I hated to see a talented golfer like Bob waste his potential.

You see, it had become common knowledge that Dylan had entered into an organic fruit and vegetable growing business. And I just couldn't imagine how he would be able to keep writing his poetry and songs, develop his golf game to its full potential (i.e., competing on the Champion's Tour), and be a full-time businessman as well.

So it didn't surprise me when he clarified the matter by saying, "*I ain't gonna work on Maggie's Farm no more!*" I took Maggie to be his organic partner, but I didn't want to pry by asking. Besides, the direction our talk had taken seemed to disrupt his rhythm and timing, golfwise, and he proceeded to shank his seven-iron approach to the green.

Naturally, Bob's shank concerned me, because the shank is the one shot in golf that infects the swing like a disease, more than a random bad chance occurrence. What's worse is that once you start shanking, it becomes very hard to stop doing it. But Dylan isn't an ordinary mortal, and, to my surprise, he had a schooled conception as to exactly what had caused this shot. In fact, for some reason, he took it upon himself at that instant to give me a little golf lesson, and I thought, "How ironically iconoclastic is that: giving someone a golf lesson right after you hit a shank!"

His point was that there was a definite correlation between the positions of the clubface at the top of the backswing and at impact.

"*You find out when you reach the top you're on the bottom,*" is how he phrased it.

"You mean if the face is too wide open at the top, the tendency is to start the hosel down at the ball instead of swinging the sweet spot toward impact?" I asked, disguising, but evidently not very well, the fact that the source of this theory was Homer Kelley's book *The Golfing Machine*.

"Somethin' like that, partner," was all he said, looking kind of weary from all this golf grilling.

In fact, exhaustion seemed to overtake him, and even though I never thought of Dylan as an optimist, he had pasted on his face an almost Mona Lisa–like smile, by which I knew that his highway blues had become the golfer's blues.

Therefore I wasn't surprised that, when on the 15th tee he reached into his bag for his three wood, he immediately let it drop back into the bag and then declared, "*I ain't even got the strength to stand up and take another shot.*"

I feared, and figured, and was, indeed, right, that my round with Dylan had come to an end. Like all golfers, though, we both wanted to find an excuse for our precipitous halting of play rather than concede to being quitters, so I pointed up at some dark clouds that had formed directly overhead, figuring he'd surely take the bait.

Yeah, "*a hard rain's a-gonna fall,*" he said, "let's hightail it outa here!"

In fact, we both knew that no precipitation was imminent—hard, soft, or otherwise.

Back in the parking lot I asked Bob where he was off to.

As he was tossing those Spanish golf boots into the trunk of his car, he said, "*I'm goin' back to New York City. I do believe I've had enough.*"

Now I've had a million friends who simultaneously love and loathe this game of golf, so I didn't completely take the implication that he might give up the game too seriously. What's more, my experience of chronically having it, losing it, and finding it, only to lose that essence of hitting golf shots solidly over and over again made me even more confident that Bob would be back.

In fact, that suspicion was confirmed the moment he slammed the trunk of his SUV shut. There, written in blue bold letters on a white bumper sticker—Bob had blocked it from my view when he was putting on his golf boots before the round—were the words "Golf: *The answer is blowin' in the wind.*"

Golf's Imponderables
(and an Answer from Jack Kerouac)

"What is the sound of one hand clapping?" is a Zen koan. Here are some golf koans to ponder.

How can both the 460-cubic-centimeter, jumbo-headed titanium and the tiny-headed hybrid/utility clubs, which measure smaller than conventional fairway metals, both be considered the easiest clubs in the bag to hit?

Why do club designers place weight around the perimeter of irons and metalwoods when the object is to strike the ball in the center of their clubfaces?

Why does swinging easy result in added distance while swinging hard results in lost distance?

What kind of wood do they use to make tees?

What's round about the layout of an eighteen-hole golf course, over which one plays a *round* of golf?

Why wasn't ambidextrous Tour player Mac O'Grady allowed to play one ball right-handed and another left-handed in a PGA two-man tournament?

What does one learn at "Tour School"?

Why is a bunker something in which one finds protection, and a sand *trap* something one tries to avoid?

Why is the long putter harder to use on long putts?

Why didn't Bobby Jones have a nickname?

How can a golfer swing on a swing "plane" made out of air?

Why isn't there an English word that rhymes with "golf"?

If golf is a game, why can't anyone recite all its rules?

If golf is "more than a game," what else is it?

What do golfers want?

Why did Johnny Carson quit golf in frustration but conclude his monologues on the *Tonight Show* with such a good-looking swing?

Why isn't there an exclusively female private country club?

If golf is a "communion with nature," why do so many courses use toxic pesticides?

Is it possible to "play" golf as a game and earn millions of dollars doing so at the same time?

If golf is a "game for old people," how do you explain Michele Wie?

Mark Twain said, "Golf is a good walk spoiled." What would he have said about playing with golf cars?

With so many "game improvement" clubs on the market, why aren't average handicaps improving?

What is the etymological root of the word *putt*?

What is the time of record of a hole in one if the ball is struck from a tee in one time zone but lands in the hole in another?

Why do virtually indestructible titanium-headed drivers need headcovers?

If the Ryder Cup is golf's most popular event, why has there never been professional team golf?

If the golf swing is a science, why can't teachers agree on the facts about how to swing the club?

With the popularity of so many heavy club training aids today, why do manufacturers continue to make actual golf clubs lighter and lighter?

If "nice guys finish last," what competitive golfer would ever want to be nice?

If golf is (in the words of Homer Kelley, author of *The Golfing Machine*) "a game for thinkers," why do people love it so passionately?

If, as a teaching tool, the "video camera doesn't lie," why can't it offer us one truth about how a golf swing feels?

Why don't golfers who "play by feel" laugh and cry on the golf course, and why aren't "mechanical" golfers' fingernails dirty?

Why do people persist in calling motorized golf cars "golf carts?"

Why isn't a persimmon-headed driver called a "woodmetal"?

If "practice makes perfect," how is perfection impossible?

Why do golfers strive for perfection and then say, "Golf is a game of misses"?

If golf is a work of art, what's its artifact?

If, as the late, great golfer and golf commentator Dave Marr once said, "golfers weren't meant to be standing over a three-foot putt for a million dollars," what should PGA Tour pros be doing on Sundays?

If a golf course is a "theatre," is the game a comedy or a tragedy?

Why is Gene Little, one of the game's all-time most fluid swingers, known as "Gene the Machine"?

Why don't people realize that Lee Trevino's nickname "The Merry Mex" is racist?

Why is it so much harder to hit the golf ball well on the golf course than on the driving range?

Why do so many teachers say they found golf's secret while only one top competitive player, Ben Hogan, ever said the same thing?

Why do golfers still feel "first tee jitters" even when they don't keep score?

Gary Player says, "You spend your whole life learning how to make a correct golf swing, and when you finally understand how, you're too old to do it." So what's the point of even trying?

If golf today is a billion-dollar-a-year industry, how could it have started with poor shepherds hitting rocks with sticks across fields of sheep?

If golfers pay "greens fees," do they play from the fairways and the rough for free?

A child once asked writer Jack Kerouac, "Why is the sky blue?" to which Kerouac answered, "The sky is blue because you ask, 'Why is the sky blue?'"

Winter Scene with Figures Playing Kolf

On an icy canvas under a sky of silver paint, with winter's weight pressing down and fields of white clouds alive with light, the brown overcoated figures play kolf, the Dutch precursor to the Scottish game of golf. The little men, with long, skirted overcoats and pilgrim-style top hats, stand and skate on their town's frozen river, a fairway of antiturf, swatting small, lopsided balls with their sticks to reach their goal with an economy of strokes. Sound familiar?

No loft is needed here, as the ball stays low and slippery, a dainty simulacrum of hockey, and if a ball did find a hole, wouldn't it be better fitted for an ice fishing pole?

In this painting the players skid through town, among buildings and trees, integrating the joys of play with the tasks of daily life in the community, unlike the courses of today that keep church, work, and play separate. Well, that's ok. Here in Pasadena's Norton Simon Museum, where the canvas hangs, all of us can see how a distant steeple pierces the filigree evening. Playing a game, and not praying, seems as good a way as any to appease cold Nature and the God or whatever it was who created her.

The wintriness of the painting is what captures our attention first, because we associate golf with every season *but* winter. We've all heard of avid, obsessed golfers, but this is ridiculous! The little men are playing below the barren, burnt-looking branches of the winter trees. It feels more like a desolate bombed-out war zone than a recreational region. A sepia haze bathes the entire canvas, again in diametric opposition of hue to golf's conventionally verdant palette.

Someone skates in the background while a man addresses the ball with an open stance, like Nicklaus over a putt. Another kolfer stands a few feet away, relaxed with his club propped under his arm, looking eerily like a golfer standing off to the side of the tee box today who watches his playing companion drive. A dog observes the action from the land, not wanting to venture one paw beyond his patch of solid footing. Hogan, they said, had ice water in his veins. He would have fit right in and felt right at home here.

With the zigzagging flow of the double-doglegging fairway, and with the huts and thatched edifices huddled close together lining the riverbank, *Winter Scene with Figures Playing Kolf* looks nothing less than a primitive golf course community inhabited by Hobbits, or other gnomelike creatures.

The icy greens look faster than Augusta National's. The dog on the riverbank watching the kolfers play evokes the famous story (and photograph) of Arnold Palmer concentrating so hard on a putt during a tournament that he didn't notice a dog running across the green.

The reflection of the light from the sky bouncing down off the icy river "kolf course" establishes the more transcendent theme of this work: spiritual illumination as the bridge between heaven and earth. Indeed, while the golfer's eye in me is drawn to the lovely anecdotal activity of the kolfers playing on the river, my inner art critic insists that the winter sky, with its clouds dramatically tinged in soft shades of reds, grays, and even blues, really wins out as the focal point of the picture.

As for a golf course, the only one that comes to mind where the sky plays such a prominently powerful role is Riviera Country Club in Pacific Palisades, just outside of LA. Built low in a basin, its eucalyptus-lined fairways create corridors that simultaneously frame the sky, or *contain* it, as if it were shoved downward into a crate walled in eucalyptus wood. Sky and fairways reflect each other there the way a chef during a cooking demonstration might set a mirror above a bowl so the audience can see the ingredients being mixed for crab cakes. Hole 17 at Riviera slopes gradually uphill over five-hundred-plus yards. Standing on the hole's tee, golfers find themselves aiming at a spot in the sky.

In this painting the wintry glow seems to have a calming effect on the kolfers, and they appear completely free of performance anxiety. It's clearly evening, so they are getting in every bit as much play as they can, which shifts the allegory into another gear—that of living life to its fullest.

The great Welsh poet Dylan Thomas implored in his famous villanelle that one should not "go gentle into that good night" but should "rage, rage against the dying of the light."

This painting offers a gentler alternative. Rather than rage, we can "play, play" through the wintry final scenes of our lives. Who knows . . . the great game of golf (or kolf), and the attitude of playfulness itself unformulated into rules for competition, may keep us young enough to endure winter's dying light until spring arrives again, as it surely will.

Source Acknowledgments